When We Won The Cup

When We Won The Cup

by
David Instone

Thomas Publications

First published in Great Britain in May, 2003, by
Thomas Publications, PO Box 17, Newport,
Shropshire, England, TF10 7WT

Acknowledgements

My thanks go to the many people who have contributed to this publication, in particular the surviving members of Alan Ashman's 1968 FA Cup-winning team. All, plus coach Stuart Williams, have been accommodating with their time and memories, in particular skipper Graham Williams, who was the players' leader 35 years ago and who, they keep being reminded, remains their leader now!

Several of Graham's photos appear within these 192 pages and I am also indebted to John Osborne's wife Jenny for her time and her loan of the many precious keepsakes she was happy for Albion fans to share in. Likewise, we thank veteran former coach Albert McPherson and supporters John Hickman and Terry Wills for their pictures, John also kindly supplying us with the programmes from all of the ties on Albion's famous FA Cup run (and several of the match tickets), so we could reproduce them.

On a commercial note, thank-you to John Homer, Philip Owen and his Nottingham-based company Minizens, West Bromwich Building Society, and Albion themselves for their considerable support with the 1968 players' reunion dinner staged to launch this book.

Finally, mine is the name on this work but my wife Liz is the one whose technical expertise has pulled it all together.

David Instone

ISBN 0 9512051 5 3

Printed and bound by Bookcraft, Midsomer Norton, Bath

Contents

Introduction

A book is unlikely ever to be written on how Manchester United won the FA Cup by beating Leicester at Wembley in 1963 or on how Liverpool were victorious in the showpiece final of the English game against Newcastle 11 seasons later. Trophies have continued to be accumulated at much too prolific a rate at Old Trafford and Anfield for any one year to stand out.

In the slipstream, though, of those leading powers, who now find themselves accompanied by Arsenal and are occasionally joined by others, a sizeable clutch of clubs have picked away at what has been left of the prizes. And, in the middle and late 1960s, West Bromwich Albion set about feasting on them.

The guest-room walls at The Hawthorns are adorned with images of days when the club not only played in the top flight for a quarter of a century but beat the elite on a regular basis. The photos should serve as inspiration for the future to those who were thrilled by the way Gary Megson's Baggies boing-boinged their way to the Premiership in the spring of 2002 and who were then left dispirited by the nine months that followed.

The Albion team who lifted the FA Cup in 1968 came from as proud a stock as any. After spectacularly winning one League Cup Final under Jimmy Hagan and then unbelievably losing another, the side passed into the gentler hands of Alan Ashman, closed in on the bigger knockout prize and ultimately delivered it on a somewhat attritional Wembley afternoon against Everton.

Four times in five seasons, Albion reached the final of a major knockout competition. In the odd year out, they reached the semi-final of the FA Cup and the quarter-final of the European Cup Winners' Cup. For four or five golden years, when going to Wembley seemed almost an annual excursion, the Baggies were a magnificent side in sudden-death football. This is the story of the most glorious of those memorable seasons.

It was an era when football was much, much different. Indeed, younger fans wouldn't recognise it as the game they watch and love today. When We Won The Cup is a tale from that bygone age when League games carried two points for a win, there were no red and yellow cards, the season-round, green-baize pitches of the modern-day game were an unimaginable luxury and rosettes and scarves were the match-day fashion rather than replica shirts.

Boing-boing hadn't been invented and there were no foreigners or even any foreign-sounding names. Actually, there was one: Albion's Nicky Krzywicki. But he was born in Flintshire, groomed in Staffordshire and British enough to go on and play for Wales!

These were the days before local radio and Ceefax. We had telegrams but no texting and the mobile phone was unheard of. The nearest thing to Internet was if you were in the crowd at Hillsborough or Elland Road and heard one of the locals shout "In t' net!" when their side were taking a corner or free-kick.

More significantly, there was no live televising of domestic matches. If you wanted to watch Law or Greaves or Baxter or, yes, Astle, Hope and Brown, you had to go and see them in the flesh. And, if you went to see them at the weekend, you knew it would be on Saturday afternoon at 3pm. Sunday was a family day and Friday night football was something with which only clubs like Tranmere experimented to try to drag in a few floating fans while Liverpool and Everton weren't playing.

If you waited to see your favourites on TV, you waited a very long time. We had Match of the Day and, in the Midlands, Star Soccer but they homed in on one or, at most, two matches and, in nearly every household in the land, they were shown on a black and white telly. The 1968 FA Cup Final was one of the first English games to be broadcast in colour.

In the absence of the prying cameras, football held a greater curiosity. You didn't know what Turf Moor or Filbert Street were like unless you went and looked for yourself. And without TV's millions, the players were not paid that much more than the fans who were watching them.

Jeff Astle packaged cigarettes at Nottingham's John Player factory before becoming established in the game. Well after his winning goal at Wembley, he was still on only £60 a week. John Kaye, Astle's first strike partner at Albion, worked in the Humberside docks before making it in football and Doug Fraser was an apprentice engineer in Glasgow.

Even skipper Graham Williams was on a basic wage of only £40 at the start of the summer of 1967 during which Alan Ashman was appointed. No-one could say they were in it just for the money - and no-one who saw them play could deny the hunger. They wore the shirt with pride, they lived in the local community and they mingled happily with the fans.

That generation have come to be remembered as the players who gave Albion some of the finest years in their history. Two League Cup Finals, an FA Cup Final, an FA Cup semi-final and a European last-eight place are testimony to that. What Baggies supporters of the early 21st century would give for achievements like that!

The club have never reached such heights since, although they have been in two more FA Cup semi-finals (1977-78 and 1981-82) and one League Cup semi-final (1981-82) and arguably had a better all-round team when the one developed by Johnny Giles, taken on by Ronnie Allen and finally polished up by Ron Atkinson chased Liverpool hard for the League Championship in the first three-quarters of 1978-79 before their challenge was buried under the snow of Britain's worst winter for a decade and a half.

By then, all but Tony Brown of the Class of 68 had left The Hawthorns and most had called time on their playing careers. Some had departed England altogether and only a few were still deriving a living from the game. The passing of the years has carried its share of anguish for the men who brought such honour to The Hawthorns.

Cancer took popular keeper John Osborne in 1998 at the age of 58. Around the same time, Jeff Astle, the life and soul of every party, started to suffer health problems and the smiling face and bubbling personality that had even lit up TV screens was rarely seen in public again. 'The King' died in January, 2002.

Reserve keeper Rick Sheppard died of a heart attack in the same month as Osborne while manager Ashman became a frail figure in the late 1990s and passed away at the end of last year. Winger Clive Clark has suffered poor health for many years and requires 24-hour care in a private residential home in North Yorkshire after the debilitating mental condition Lorsakow's Syndrome wiped away his short-term memory.

Among several of the others, the scars of so many years in football, in an era when pain-killing injections routinely provided short-term relief and hid longer-term problems, are clearly evident.

Centre-half John Talbut, who had a heart attack in 2000, has a replacement left knee as the result of arthritis. Multi record-breaker Tony Brown has been fitted with two new hips and Ian Collard also has a replacement hip following the arthritis discovery that ended his playing days.

It's ironic that Graham Lovett, who suffered two appalling car accidents during his football career, is now happy and well in his new life in Spain. By coincidence, he lives only a couple of miles away from his former team-mate Dennis Clarke, injury having forced both out of the game at the peak age of 26.

Life has by no means been kind to all of Ashman's men outside football. In it, though, they were winners - and this is the fullest-ever account of their climb to hero status. This is the story recounting how they earned the right to tell their grandchildren all about 'When We Won The Cup.'

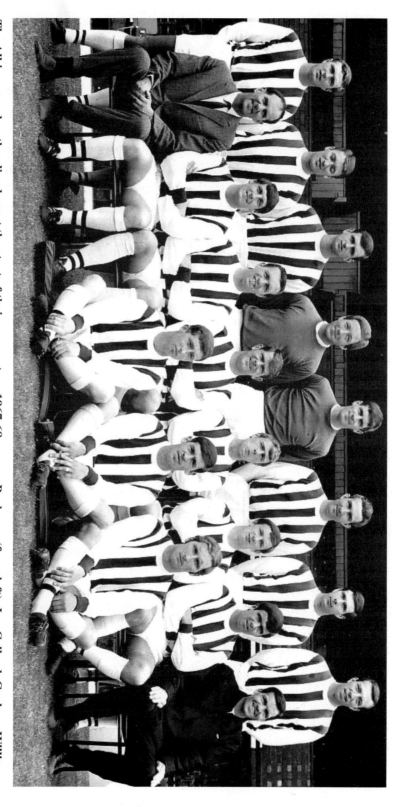

The Albion squad as they lined up at the start of their momentous 1967-68 season. Back row (from left): Ian Collard, Graham Williams, Eddie Colquhoun, Rick Sheppard, John Osborne, Stan Jones, Ray Fairfax, John Talbut. Middle: Alan Ashman (manager), Tony Brown, Jeff Astle, John Kaye, Clive Clark, Ken Foggo, Bobby Hope, Albert McPherson (trainer). Front: Gerry Howshall, Doug Fraser, Dennis Clarke.

A Rich Cup Pedigree

West Bromwich Albion and FA Cup success had been familiar bed-fellows for decades before Graham Williams hoisted that gleaming silverware above his head on the late afternoon of May 18, 1968. Their long-held tag as the proudest of fighters in sudden-death football was merely underlined by one magnificent connection from Jeff Astle's unfavoured left foot.

Albion are not a Coventry City or an Ipswich Town; in other words, a club who lifted the Cup once and then retreated again to the very fringes of the chase for the biggest knockout honour in the domestic game. They won it once way back when in the early years and they went back and won it again and again. They are multi-winners.

This book provides the full, in-depth story of how the Cup came to rest in the Black Country 35 years ago. It has not been back since and we wonder, amid the increasing stranglehold the superpowers are establishing, when and whether it will do so again. The long wait, though, has added enchantment to the tale and made the achievements of Alan Ashman's men all the more special.

Albion were, quite simply, the best team in the country in knockout football from 1966 to 1970, yet their heroic deeds didn't spring from nowhere. Their successes were the pinnacle of achievement from a tremendously talented, although at times frustratingly flawed group of players who developed a legendary spirit of togetherness as they emblazoned the club's name around the world.

And, as background to this detailed account of triumph in the face of much adversity, it is worth reflecting on the tremendous Cup-fighting record that was already part of the Hawthorns fabric long before Williams, Astle and the rest arrived on the scene. Only once in their 125-year history have the Baggies lifted the League Championship. But the Cups? They have always been a different matter altogether.

Wembley 68 was the club's tenth appearance in the final and, by neat symmetry, the split of wins and losses adds up to 5-5. Throw in another nine losing outings in the semi-final (for many years, Albion had the record for most appearances in the last four) and it's plain to see that they have never been a club to be taken lightly away from the treadmill of gathering points.

As founder members of the Football League and inhabitants of one of the original hotbeds of the sport, they did some of their trophy plundering very early on, although their initial FA Cup excursions were unrewarding. Having run up the cricket-like score of 26-0 against Coseley in a Birmingham Cup first-round tie in 1882-83, they were less successful when they first became eligible to play in the national competition in 1883, losing 2-0 at home to Wednesbury Town in their first-ever tie.

Defeat at the sixth-round stage at home to Blackburn in front of a record 16,393 crowd the following year represented a major improvement and it was the Lancashire club who were to become their first opponents in a final on April 3, 1886 - at a time when Albion had lost only one tie out of 14 in the competition going back to two and a half years earlier.

Their fine Cup record was to stretch even further and become only two defeats in 26 games played from October, 1885, to March, 1889, and they won ten matches in a row in the competition from October 15, 1887. But the Blackburn final had no happy ending. The clubs drew 0-0 at The Oval before Rovers won the replay 2-0 at Derby's county cricket ground to lift the trophy for a still unmatched third successive season.

Albion had been drawn at home in the earlier five rounds, beating Aston Unity, Wednesbury Old Athletic, Wolves, Old Carthusians and Old Westminsters, and then making the short semi-final journey to put four past Short Heath at Aston. Eighty-two years before Birmingham (the name by which Short Heath later became known) were beaten at Villa Park by a side who went on to defeat Everton at Wembley, at least Albion had earned the honour of being the first Midlands club to reach the final.

They were back the following year in the first all-Midlands final, only to suffer more disappointment as Aston Villa beat them 2-0. But it was only a further 12 months on that it proved to be third time lucky as hot favourites Preston, known as the Invincibles, were defeated 2-1.

Albion's team contained Billy Bassett - a right-winger who was to win 16 England caps and serve the club as a player and administrator for no fewer than 50 years - and Ezra Horton, a right-half who played in all of the club's first 36 FA Cup ties. The duo did much to ensure their side were the first to win the Cup with 11 English-born players.

Preston, like their conquerors, were among the 12 founder members of the Football League in 1888, so it was perhaps fitting that their meeting should produce the first capacity crowd (18,904) in English football. And Albion, in a manner that became their trademark, continued to make more of an impact in the shorter version of the game than the drawn-out one.

Having reached six semi-finals in seven years, they were back in the final in 1891-92 for the last staging of the showpiece at The Oval. Again, they finished their journey in style, this time 3-0 against Aston Villa, at the end of a season in which they made history as the only club to win the Cup and have to secure re-election to the League.

The pendulum swung back to their neighbours in 1895, though, with a first minute goal seeing off the Baggies at the new final venue of Crystal Palace. In a far cry from the security measures of today, the silverware was put on show in a shop window in Aston and promptly snatched, never to be recovered. Villa had to find £25 for a replacement as their supporters gloated that they had had the Cup stolen as many times as Albion had won it!

It was to be 35 years - coincidentally the exact time span we're looking at now since Albion last won the FA Cup - until the club were to get their hands on the new version. In the meantime, they lost in semi-finals against Tottenham at Villa Park in 1900-01 and Everton at Bolton in 1906-07, and 1-0 in extra-time of a replayed final against Barnsley at Sheffield in 1912 after a 0-0 draw in the original game at Crystal Palace.

They had the major consolation of winning the League Championship in 1919-20 for what is still the only time in their history but were to suffer their third painful experience of relegation before lifting the Cup again. That success was in the memorable 1930-31 campaign, which ended with Albion becoming the first club to win promotion and the FA Cup in the same season.

The ball flashes across Albion's goalmouth to safety in their 1931 FA Cup Final victory against local rivals Birmingham at Wembley. The Baggies' success capped a tremendous season in which they also won promotion. They were the last Second Division side to lift the Cup until Sunderland 42 years later. Picture courtesy of Associated Newspapers.

Albion, in unfamiliar dark shirts, on the attack during their 4-2 defeat against Sheffield Wednesday in the 1935 FA Cup Final. Picture courtesy of Associated Newspapers.

The 2-1 victory, this time at Wembley, was even sweeter for supporters as it came against Birmingham in a game settled by goals from the renowned W G Richardson in the middle of each half. Blues controversially had a goal disallowed for offside before the Duke of Gloucester handed to Tommy Glidden the trophy that an estimated 150,000 fans turned out to see on the team's homecoming the next day.

Albion were riding high in the early 1930s with four successive top-ten top-flight finishes, although their 1931-32 Cup defence was ended by Villa at the first hurdle. They didn't have to wait long for more joy, though, and were back at Wembley in 1935. Odd-goal home victories against Port Vale and Preston came either side of slaughters of Sheffield United (7-1) and Stockport (5-0), then Bolton were beaten 2-0 at Stoke in a semi-final replayed after a 1-1 draw at Leeds.

But Albion's hopes of a fourth winning of the Cup evaporated as a patched-up side - Tommy Glidden was not fully fit after a cartilage operation and inside-right Joe Carter was also struggling with a knee problem that had prevented him playing in the League since early March - were surprisingly beaten 4-2 by Sheffield Wednesday.

Albion were one win short of another final appearance in 1936-37 when they crashed 4-1 to old rivals Preston in the semis at Highbury, the name of Arsenal having been etched in Hawthorns history books in the previous round when the

3-1 victory over the Gunners was watched by the biggest ever crowd at the ground, 64,815.

The disappointment of that aborted Cup journey was nothing, though, compared with the despair of relegation again in 1938 and the start of a big-time exile that, courtesy of the Second World War, stretched to 11 years before being ended by Jack Smith's team in 1949.

Smith had moved on to Reading and been succeeded by Jesse Carver and then Vic Buckingham by the time Albion were booking their next visit to the twin towers. When they embarked on their 1953-54 Cup campaign with a 1-0 win at home to Chelsea, they had not been past the fifth round for five years but looked the part as they rattled on with goal-filled victories at home to Rotherham, Newcastle and Tottenham.

At the same time, Albion were vying with Wolves for the Championship in a League head-to-head rivalled for its all-Black Country drama only by the race for automatic promotion from the Nationwide First Division in the spring of 2002. The Baggies were well placed to become the first club to win the coveted double as the respective finishing lines came into view but their luck held in one of the competitions and ran out in the other.

Many observers had them down as fortunate to hang on for their 2-1 semi-final victory over Third Division Port Vale at Villa Park - sealed by goals by Jimmy Dudley and Potteries-born Ronnie Allen - but that kind rub of the green provided a stark contrast to the setbacks that befell them with injuries and international calls to several key players during the Championship run-in.

An unusual image of the 1954 FA Cup Final at a stifling Wembley as keeper Jim Sanders (left) and his skipper Len Millard reach for the oxygen masks at half-time in the 3-2 win over Preston.

Albion finished second in the League but rounded off a magnificent season by winning 3-2 in a thrilling FA Cup Final over Preston. Allen, as in the semi-final, kept cool to make it 2-2 from one of the most famous penalties in Cup Final history, his much-photographed second goal of the day being followed by a Frank Griffin winner three minutes from the end.

The club's reign as Cup holders was ended by Charlton in a fourth-round tie at The Hawthorns and defeats in successive seasons against Birmingham and Villa at advanced stages, the second occasion in a 1956-57 semi-final replay at St Andrew's, ensured there would be no more Cup Finals for now. Indeed, Wembley remained a distant dream as the club followed their 1958 sixth-round replay defeat at an emotional post-Munich Old Trafford with some undignified exits.

In 1960, Graham Williams made his FA Cup debut in a home win over Plymouth and so became the first piece in the 1968 jigsaw. He also played in a third-round loss at Lincoln 12 months later, in an embarrassing 3-0 crash at Bolton in 1965-66 and in the 5-0 fourth-round beating at Leeds the following season that still stands as the club's heaviest-ever defeat in the competition.

By then, the excellent reputation Albion had developed in knockout football had found another outlet via the League Cup. Twice in just over a year, they contested the final of the initially shunned new competition and received civic recognition when representatives of their boardroom, management and playing staff were invited to the Mayor's Parlour in West Bromwich as a thank-you for the prestige the club had brought the town.

Now, at the dawn of 1967-68, Albion were once again at the start of the long road to Wembley. They had plenty to live up to after the successes of bygone Baggies teams but they had new direction with the appointment of Alan Ashman as manager. They were all assembled and ready to go.

Alan Ashman

Albion's continuing success in cup football in 1966-67 was not enough to keep Jimmy Hagan in a job. The goal-scoring Sheffield United legend had brought League Cup glory to The Hawthorns in 1965-66 and took the club on an exciting defence that ended in a shock defeat in the final against QPR the following season. He had also given them their first taste of Europe.

But relegation had been a threat for much of 1966-67 and the Hawthorns board were concerned at the frequent rifts between Hagan and his squad. Not that they were anything new. In the early months of the manager's reign, the club made major unwanted headlines when players went on strike in protest at not being allowed to wear tracksuit bottoms for training on cold mornings.

Around the same time, Hagan famously slammed his car into the wrong gear when negotiating the training-ground car park, hurtled into the adjacent canal and had to be rescued from a watery grave by his players, one of whom, keeper Tony Millington, was left puffing and panting at the unexpected exertion. "Millington, you're not fit," the manager barked from his rather vulnerable position. "Extra training!"

The dressing-room mood remained turbulent despite the 1965-66 winning of a first trophy in 12 years and was reflected the following season in a stream of transfer requests. Senior pros Jeff Astle, Graham Williams, Stan Jones and Ken Foggo were joined on the want-away list by reserves Rick Sheppard and Gerry Howshall, although all six ultimately outstayed their boss.

Nevertheless, the club's directors decided it was time for change at the helm once top-flight football had been secured for a 19th consecutive season in the spring of 1967. An outstanding run-in reaped 18 points from 11 games but was not enough to prevent the axe falling on Hagan - boss since April, 1963 - a few days after a 3-1 home win over West Ham.

Only a couple of matches remained in the League programme and it wasn't long into the summer that the search for a replacement threw up a successor. Wolves' former Albion star Ronnie Allen was a hot early tip and Matt Busby (Manchester United), Bill Shankly (Liverpool), Bill Nicholson (Tottenham), Harry Catterick (Everton), Ron Greenwood (West Ham) and Tommy Docherty (Chelsea) were the leading managerial names of the day.

Don Revie (Leeds) and the Joe Mercer-Malcolm Allison liaison at Manchester City were just about to flourish in a big way but, as they had done with the recruitment of Hagan, who had cut his managerial teeth with Third Division Peterborough, Albion moved instead for a man who had made his

This is how I want it done - new Albion manager Alan Ashman introduces himself to his inherited coaches (from left) Jimmy Dunn, Stuart Williams and Albert McPherson.

mark in the lower divisions, in this case at the northern outpost of Carlisle.

It would be pure pretence to say that the players left behind by Hagan and in many instances signed by him were beside themselves with excitement when one-time chicken farmer George Alan Ashman was unveiled as their new boss on May 23, 1967. They knew little about him and they knew little about the walled town he came from.

The Cumbrian club traditionally occupied a place in the lower divisions and Brunton Park did not feature on Albion's list of professional destinations. "The only reason Carlisle was ever mentioned in the dressing-room," one player said, "was because the Scots lads used to call it the last stopping-off point in England on their way back home."

But Ashman had seen to it that unfashionable little Carlisle were now a shade more fashionable and not quite as little. His job tenure in the border country had run parallel to that of Hagan at The Hawthorns (1963 to 1967) and things were stirring in the shadow of Hadrian's Wall. Relegation to the bottom division in 1964 was followed by back-to-back promotions and by two years of consolidation in the Second Division, only one grade below the level Albion had graced for 18 years.

Ashman's name was consequently on the lips of more than a few directors who had found food for thought in the way he had given a club from the backwaters the taste for bigger and better things. Albion had long been feasting at the game's top table but chairman Jim Gaunt and his board had found a boss who, at 38, was hungry for success and who, they believed, was capable of serving it up.

Hagan, ironically a hero of Ashman's because of his star status at Sheffield United - the club the latter was to play a few reserve games for - was an interesting act to follow. He had never been popular with the squad but he had their utmost respect. One cherished cap for England and a further 16 outings in wartime international football had helped see to that.

Stories about how he used to 'send off' a player in training so he could take their place in practice matches are legendary among his staff. So is the ability he would show once he was on the pitch. Even in his mid and late 40s, he impressed all and sundry with the way he played and competed against athletes barely half his age.

Hagan wasn't a nasty man - indeed, away from the pressure of games, he was seen as enjoyable and entertaining company. But he had crossed swords with too many of his players for the relationship to be affectionate and his regime could accurately be said to be harsh. He was a disciplinarian whose ways bordered on dictatorial.

The talented players he bequeathed Alan Ashman were at times a little shell-shocked under his management but were about to discover that natural ability could be coaxed out as well as drummed out. They were more than ready for the gentler ways and arm-round-the-shoulder treatment they were about to receive from his successor.

"Jimmy had been a great player but, as a manager, he was a bit like Brian Clough," says Daily Mail sports writer Ray Matts, then Albion correspondent for the Wolverhampton-based Express & Star. "He was irascible. He was set in his ways and he had this stern approach. He was incredibly well respected but he wasn't well liked among the players.

"There was always a distance between them and him. They would train forever and then, when they were thinking about lunch and home, he would start a five-a-side game, in which he would invariably be both the referee and the man-of-the-match!

"Having said that, I enjoyed being with him. I used to join him for lunch because my office was just along the road from a working man's café that he often used on West Bromwich high street. He would have a cup of tea and a Wagon Wheel and be quite happy talking with you on any aspect of football. You can't imagine Sir Alex Ferguson or Arsene Wenger doing that!

"Alan Ashman was a quieter man and would often be sucking a polo mint as he spoke to you. He was a thinker and, when he first came into the club, he had the good sense to realise that the team already in place were good. He knew he didn't have to rush in and change everything. Above all, the players genuinely liked him and it was like a thaw after the Cold War. A gelling or bonding took place with him in charge and it really bore fruit during the 1967-68 FA Cup run.

"He let the players get on with it and didn't make waves. He wasn't a fool. He was astute and he recognised, like everyone in the football world did, that Albion's players had the ability to produce sensational, almost unbelievable, football while also being capable of suffering the occasional defeat that was absolutely crackers."

As a centre-forward, Rotherham-born Ashman topped the Third Division North scorers in 1953-54 with 30 goals for Carlisle, having joined them for what was then a club record £5,500 from Nottingham Forest. He spent seven years as a player at Brunton Park before moving into coaching and cutting his management teeth with nearby Penrith, a Northern League club he steered to the quarter-final of the FA Amateur Cup.

Alongside the running of the part-timers, his upbringing in Yorkshire and closeness to the Lake District had seen to it that he always kept some sturdy boots in the back of his car so he could indulge his love of walking. In Cumbria, he also worked at a farm raising turkeys and birds in batteries, where he was fortunate to have a Carlisle United director as his boss. The link led to him being appointed manager of his former club in 1963 and he had four years in charge before Albion went calling.

The Hawthorns board had received applications from other possibly more

One of those 'crackers' results - John Osborne, with Doug Fraser as company in between two attackers, is beaten as Reading shock Albion 3-1 at Elm Park in the 1967-68 League Cup. Picture courtesy of Reading Evening Post.

fancied candidates but not from available men. "It wasn't our policy to chase people under contract," said chairman Jim Gaunt. "That left us looking for an up-and-coming young manager who had proved himself in a lower sphere. After many days' thinking and talking, Alan Ashman's was the one name that kept cropping up in the discussions. He was the one we decided to go for."

Ironically as things were to turnout, Albion made their move on the eve of the 1967 FA Cup Final between Tottenham and Chelsea. A meeting was arranged for the Saturday morning in a private suite of the luxurious Park Lane Hotel, where chairman and manager were to return in joyous mood 12 months later.

The football spotlight being nothing like today, especially in terms of TV exposure, Gaunt had no idea what Ashman looked like. But both were invited to the Friday night Football Writers' Association Player of the Year awards do and the chairman said: "For all I knew, Alan might have been sitting at the next table. I had never set eyes on him and had no idea which one he was.

"But we had our meeting in private the following morning and a hall porter from the hotel and some of the other staff were 'in' on the secret. They kept it quiet for us. One thing we learned about Alan straightaway was that he was a very tough negotiator; a trait that stood him in good stead as a manager. He knew exactly what he was worth and he fully intended to get it."

Ashman might have been a tough figure to face across a table. He didn't easily recognise a losing cause on the field of play, either. An accomplished cricketer, he once hit a six and a four off the last two balls to win a Minor Counties match for Cumberland that was talked about in the area for many years.

After the initial meeting, Gaunt and Ashman quickly reconvened, this time in the company of the manager's wife. A deal was struck, albeit with the condition that there would be no announcement about his appointment at The Hawthorns until he had had time to tell the Carlisle chairman in person that he was leaving.

Gaunt knew he was dealing with a gentleman as well as a man of substance and added in the latter stages of the 1967-68 FA Cup run: "That insistence was typical of Alan, who we have come to know and respect. He is a deep thinker, fair-minded and very much a method man. He believes in trying to build up the lesser players and make the good ones even better."

The move to The Hawthorns was a definite step-up for Ashman. He was leaving a club who traditionally occupied the lower divisions and joining one whose stay in the top flight was to become exceeded only by Arsenal and Manchester United. "I had no second thoughts about joining Albion," he said. "It seemed to be the logical thing to do when Jim Gaunt approached me. I had never seen the club play but I knew the players by reputation and knew they were good players."

It was the perfect appointment on the part of the club's board because the new man was good at the aspects of the job that his predecessor had struggled with. He was an excellent man-manager and therefore well placed to extract the best from the rich raw materials Hagan had left behind. If he didn't unduly rock the boat and seek to overhaul the squad, Albion could look forward to some fruitful years.

Hagan had proved himself to be a master with the cheque-book. Albion had never been seen as big spenders or a particularly glitzy club but, with the funds made available to him, he had landed Jeff Astle for £25,000, John Kaye for £45,000, John Osborne for £10,000, John Talbut for £33,000 and Doug Fraser for £23,000. They were the backbone of the FA Cup winning team and their combined first-team appearance tally for the club was to top 1,550 - an average of more than 300 per man.

Ashman's own transfer dealings brought mixed results. Although he spent brilliantly when signing the club's third highest all-time appearance-maker John Wile for only £32,000 from Peterborough in 1970 and was the manager when Alistair Robertson was brought south as a youngster from Scotland, other deals were to have question marks against them.

He splashed out what were then big sums for Ronnie Rees, Colin Suggett, Danny Hegan and Allan Glover to only modest effect and the same could be said when keeper Jim Cumbes and winger George McVitie came and went without making the big impact of their predecessors..

One knack both managers clearly had, though, was the seamless blooding of talented young players. Hagan had groomed Nick Krzywicki and Kenny Stephens, plus Wembley 1968 finalists Tony Brown, Graham Lovett, Ian Collard and Dennis Clarke, while Ashman was to introduce talents such as Asa Hartford, Len Cantello, Ray Wilson, Alan Merrick and Ally Robertson from the reserve ranks.

There was another likeness. Neither could translate thrilling cup success into any significant reversal of the club's League fortunes, although subsequent managers, boards and generations of fans would have been quite happy with the final top-flight placings of 14th, 10th, 14th, 6th and 13th achieved by Hagan, and those of 8th, 10th, 16th and 17th with which Ashman followed up.

"Alan Ashman was so good at man-management," said forward-turned-defender John Kaye. "He knew just how to treat everyone. You felt relaxed with him and never under pressure. Jimmy Hagan, away from football, was as nice a bloke as you could hope to meet. At a social function, he was good company, a good laugh. But he was a different man when his mind switched to football.

"The players had ability but Jimmy wanted everybody to be like him - and he was fantastic in training, even at his age. He couldn't comprehend that not everybody was going to be as capable as him. Alan also liked to join in the five-a-sides but tactics weren't such a big thing in those days as they are today. Control it, pass it, know where to go - that was his philosophy.

"And his main belief was that if you were happy, you had more chance of being successful. He used to treat us all as human beings and showed a lot of commonsense. I can't ever remember him losing his temper. He was very popular with the lads and always used to encourage us."

Graham Williams served both managers as skipper and was to perform one of the readings at Ashman's funeral in December, 2002. There, he spoke of 'the dreaded polo' - the offer of a mint to a player who was being taken on one side. "Alan was eating polos all the time and there was always a joke that, if he offered you one, he was about to tell you he was dropping you! He was a gentle,

Long faces as Jimmy Hagan (left) takes his players' dinner order on arrival at their hotel on the eve of the 1966-67 League Cup Final against QPR. The smiles soon returned with the appointment of Alan Ashman. Picture courtesy of Associated Newspapers.

nice man and I don't think he found it very easy to break bad news."

The manager nevertheless insisted on being called 'Boss' and occasionally showed his harder side. He always regarded one of his greatest feats as Albion boss to be the unbeaten record his team clung to on their tour of East Africa in the summer of 1968. With each passing 90 minutes in what became a quite violent series of matches, he reminded his side they were playing for the honour of England - and was a proud man when they headed home with a six-game record of three wins and three draws.

Coach Stuart Williams was generally the more outgoing partner in the think-tank team. As the go-between in the necessary gap separating management and players, he enjoyed a good night-out with his boys when the time was right. His international background with Wales added to his charisma and the chemistry between he and Ashman was one of the key ingredients.

It was on the African tour that Ashman also showed himself able to let down what bit of hair he had! In the Kenyan capital of Nairobi, where Albion beat the national team 2-1 and 4-3, the players were summoned to see their manager on one occasion after their 7.30am training session.

"We thought we were in for a spot of bother because we had been out for a drink the night before without Alan knowing," John Kaye added. "It was the night before a match and we feared he had clocked us on the way back in. After training, though, he said: 'You know, we've been out here for more than two weeks now and we haven't had a night-out yet. We'll meet after the match tonight in the Swiss Cottage at quarter to midnight.' And we did. Needless to say, we had another good evening."

But Ashman knew when and where to draw the line and that once proved to be in the confines of the team's famous FA Cup retreat, the Prince of Wales Hotel at Southport. Overhearing a drinks order being made by a waiter at the bar, the manager's ears immediately pricked up as he recognised the room number as belonging to two of his players.

He intercepted the order, informed the hotel staff he would be dealing with it personally and awaited with interest the reaction of the duo in question as he knocked their door. When the shocked players greeted their manager, who was standing there with an empty drinks tray and a dark look, they were told in no uncertain terms: "Right, that will be a week's wages, each!"

Right-hand man Stuart Williams made it his business to get close to the players he was coaching day after day and appreciated the freedom Ashman gave him on the training ground. Only occasionally did the manager rein him in via minor adjustments to his routines. For the most part, Williams provided the tactical input, Ashman was the overseer and the two blended perfectly.

"Alan's dry sense of humour made him lovely company for a night out,"

Williams said. "But, at work, he was like a mother hen, looking over his flock, caring. He told me from the start I would be doing the training and he would watch, just giving his opinion if he thought something wasn't right. That didn't happen very often and I had a big say in what the players did. That also got me very close to them.

"I was a bit more outgoing than Alan and occasionally used to join the players for a night out, usually on a Monday well away from any matches. I would stay for a couple of drinks before saying: 'Right, I'll be on my way but you stay for a bit longer if you like. Tonight, I have been a lovely bloke. Tomorrow, I will be a bastard!'" It is well recognised that footballers who have an evening out are put through it the next day to compensate.

As an experienced Welsh international, Williams was more widely known in the game than his boss. Only with FA Cup success did national recognition come for Ashman, and ex-Birmingham Evening Mail sports reporter Dennis Shaw recalls: "People used to mix Alan up with the former Norwich manager, Ron Ashman, and we used to tease him by asking whether he had any pictures of himself as a player. Everyone knew he had had a modest playing career."

It didn't concern Alan Ashman that his profile was relatively low. He was no Bill Shankly in terms of character and he had a long way to go to be mentioned in the same breath as the Nicholsons, Busbys and Revies. But Albion's FA Cup progress and largely impressive League form in 1967-68 were to bolster his flourishing reputation and underline his move south from Carlisle as a very good one.

The Cast

John Osborne: Born at Barlborough in Derbyshire and signed by Albion for £10,000 at the age of 26 in January, 1967. Had previously played 110 League games for Chesterfield, emerging from the famous goalkeeping academy that spawned Gordon Banks and Bob Wilson. Won two England schoolboy caps as an outfield player, against the Republic of Ireland and Scotland, contesting midfield supremacy in the first of them with Johnny Giles - later to become his boss at The Hawthorns. Arrived too late to play in the 1966-67 League Cup run but soon became a first-team regular and matured into one of the best and most eccentric keepers in Albion's history. Nickname: Ossie.

Doug Fraser: Born in Busby, in the Eaglesham district of Glasgow, in 1941 and a late convert to a game in which he showed himself to be a fine passer as well as a tough tackler. Cut his teeth in professional football with Aberdeen, with whom he played 70 games in the early 1960s, before leaving behind home and those big games against Celtic and Rangers. Joined faraway Albion in the autumn of 1963 for £23,000 and played at wing-half for much of his career but was converted to a right-back during the 1967-68 FA Cup run, underlining his leadership credentials with a spell as skipper. Nickname: Fraz or Dougie.

Graham Williams: Born in Hellan, North Wales, in 1938 and aborted his boyhood ambitions to become a boxer so he could concentrate on football, initially as a goalkeeper. Then became a left-winger and finally a left-back, making his first-team debut in 1955 but playing only a bit-part for several seasons until his rival and 'tutor' Stuart Williams departed to Southampton in 1959-60. Had already appeared in more than 300 games for the club and over 20 for his country when he highlighted his long career, much of it as the club's skipper, by leading Albion in their 1967-68 FA Cup run. Nickname: Willie.

Tony Brown: Oldham-born lover of Manchester United who turned down the chance of an apprenticeship at Manchester City to pursue a career at the 'friendlier' West Bromwich Albion. Moved to The Hawthorns in 1961 and overcame bouts of homesickness to make his debut at Ipswich in 1963, ten days after Doug Fraser, and establish himself as a first-team regular well before the club's cup glory years of the late 1960s. Often played as a right-winger or inside-right in his earlier years but successfully converted to a goal-scoring right-half (attacking midfielder) in 1967-68. Nickname: Bomber or Boner.

John Talbut: Commanding centre-half who was born in Oxford in 1940 but grew up in his parents' native north east, from where he was spotted and signed by Burnley. Made his senior debut at Turf Moor in the late 1950s but played only a few games in the side who pipped Wolves to the League Championship in 1959-60 and missed out on a place in their losing line-up in the 1962 FA Cup Final against Tottenham. Chalked up 138 League games for Burnley before being taken to The Hawthorns by Jimmy Hagan for the unusual fee of £33,000 in the winter of 1966-67 and emerging as an ever-present in the 1967-68 season. Nickname: Big T.

John Kaye: Craggy forward-turned-defender who was born in Goole in 1940 and played 77 League games for Scunthorpe before becoming Albion's club record signing at £44,750 in 1963. Named in Sir Alf Ramsey's provisional squad for the 1966 World Cup Finals but omitted from the final 22 and ultimately had to be content with two appearances in the Football League representative side, in the first of which he scored twice in a 5-0 win over the League of Ireland. Overcame early injury problems at The Hawthorns to play 121 out of 126 League games up to the 1968 FA Cup Final. Nickname: Yorky.

Graham Lovett: Exciting young wing-half, born in the 'Blues' territory of Sheldon in 1947, and good enough to overcome some early obstacles in his career. Used to spend his spare time watching Birmingham train but hopes of hitting the big time himself seemed to be sinking when once told he was not big enough to make a good footballer. Was given another opportunity and took it, making his Albion debut at home to Chelsea in December, 1964, before establishing himself with 36 League appearances in the following season. Then came the first of the two cruel slices of misfortune he suffered on the roads. Nickname: Shuv.

Ian Collard: Skilful midfielder and occasional left-back born in the north-east in 1947 and blooded for the first time at home to Burnley in September, 1964, two years after he joined Albion straight from school. Showed signs of establishing himself at The Hawthorns by playing 38 League and cup games for the club in 1966-67, including the fateful League Cup Final against QPR. But had another frustrating spell on the sidelines in 1967-68 before re-emerging in the final third of the campaign and stepping up his challenge for a place in the Wembley line-up.

Jeff Astle: Born in the Nottinghamshire mining village of Eastwood in 1942 and went on to feature among the biggest idols in Albion history as well as becoming one of English football's finest centre-forwards of the time. At one stage rejected by his first professional club Notts County but came again and formed an awesome double act with Tony Hateley before Jimmy Hagan's talent-spotting instincts 'reeled' him in. Cost Albion a bargain £25,000 in September, 1964, and scored 20 goals or more in each of his first five full seasons at The Hawthorns. His goals made him synonymous with the glory of 1968. Nickname: Big Jeff or The King.

Bobby Hope: Described by Jeff Astle as 'the most outstanding player in the team' and the man who created many of the centre-forward's goals. Born in Bridge of Allan, Stirlingshire, in 1943 and proved to be the most successful of a batch of four youngsters sent down from north of the border in 1959. Had to wait only until the age of 16 for his senior debut against Arsenal and became a first-choice selection almost as soon as he switched from no 8 to no 10 in the second half of 1962-63. Won international honours at various age groups and helped Albion win the League Cup Final in 1965-66 and reach the final the year after. Nickname: Hopey.

Clive Clark: Born in Leeds in 1940 and had a trial with Huddersfield before scoring seven goals in 58 League games for QPR. Cost Albion only £17,000 when signed by them in 1961 and had an excellent career at The Hawthorns, becoming second only to Tommy Glidden in the list of great goal-scoring wingers at the club. Played and scored in the League Cup Final triumph over West Ham and included a brace against QPR in the 1967 League Cup Final among his haul of 93 goals in 358 matches, including one or more in every round of that competition. Described by Jeff Astle as 'a brilliant little winger who was frightened of no-one.' Nickname: Chippy.

Dennis Clarke: Born in Stockton, near Middlesbrough, in 1948 and joined Albion in 1963 straight from school, making his senior debut in a 3-0 Boxing Day win at home to Tottenham on Boxing Day, 1966. Recognised mainly as a full-back, although he played at centre-half against QPR at the twin towers in 1967 because the unlucky Stan Jones was deemed unfit for the League Cup Final for the second consecutive season. Was the youngest member of the triumphant FA Cup squad and lucky enough to include two Wembley Cup Final appearances in a modest tally of first-team outings. Nickname: Clarkey.

Eddie Colquhoun: Born in Edinburgh in 1945 and a right-back or central defender who cost £25,000 when he joined Albion a few months before going

27

on a world tour with Scotland in the summer of 1967. Previously appeared in 81 League games for Bury and made his Hawthorns debut in a 2-2 home draw against Sunderland, reeling off a run of 12 successive League appearances that spring, although he had to sit out the League Cup Final against QPR as he was cup-tied and played only in the last game of the club's Inter Cities Fairs Cup campaign - at home to Bologna. Was almost ever-present in 1967-68 until misfortune struck in a big way.

Kenny Stephens: Born in Bristol in 1946 and picked up in 1962 by Albion, for whom he made his first-team debut in a League Cup tie at home to Manchester City in October, 1966. Scored the first goal in that 4-2 third-round success and played his first League game for the club in a draw at Sunderland the following Saturday. Appeared in 13 out of 14 top-flight games in the autumn of 1967 and was hailed as a right-winger of some ability. But was still seen as a fringe player as the FA Cup journey began. Nickname: Kenjy.

Nicky Krzywicki: Born in Flintshire in 1947, the son of a Polish paratroop instructor. Joined Albion in 1962 from youth football in the Staffordshire Moorlands town of Leek and was sweeping the dressing-room floor when given the news he was to make his senior debut in December, 1964, against a Fulham side containing Bobby Robson, Rodney Marsh, George Cohen and Johnny Haynes. Although capped by Wales at under-23 international in 1966-67, first-team chances on Albion's right wing came slowly but he hit a purple patch of three goals in five games - all away - in the month immediately prior to the start of the 1967-68 FA Cup run. Nickname: Kryzy.

Rick Sheppard: Spectacular, if occasionally error-prone reserve goalkeeper who was born in Bristol in 1945. Moved to The Hawthorns straight from school in 1960 and had to wait until emerging from the shadows of Ray Potter and making his debut in the 1965-66 campaign. Played extensively in the League Cup during the club's journey to the finals in 1966 and 1967, including the fateful Wembley meeting with QPR in the latter. But remained frustrated by lack of opportunities as John Osborne came in above him and restricted him to long spells of reserve-team football. Nickname: Dick.

Colchester United
1967-68

Official programme 6d.

COLCHESTER UNITED FOOTBALL
CLUB   TELEPHONE   74042

Saturday, January 27

COLCHESTER 1
Stratton 8
ALBION 1
Brown 38 (pen)

COLCHESTER   V   ALBION

COLCHESTER		ALBION
Ernie Adams	1	John Osborne
Denis Mochan	2	Eddie Colquhoun
Brian Hall	3	Graham Williams
Derek Travis	4	Tony Brown
Duncan Forbes	5	John Talbut
Bobby Blackwood	6	Doug Fraser
Terry Price	7	Nick Krzywicki
John Mansfield	8	John Kaye
Reg Stratton	9	Jeff Astle
Tom McKechnie	10	Bobby Hope
John Martin	11	Clive Clark
(for McKechnie, 82) Peter Bullock	12	Graham Lovett (for Krzywicki, HT)

Attendance: 15,981
Ref: A Jones (Ormskirk)

A Lucky Reprieve

The dust was just settling on a high-profile 1967-68 Christmas and New Year programme when Albion learned that their FA Cup run was to begin at just the sort of venue they had come to dread visiting. Colchester away was anything but an assignment to spread fear into a side from the upper reaches of the top flight. But this was West Bromwich Albion - brilliant or bemusing depending on how the occasion found them.

Colchester, at the time, were 16th in the old Third Division and destined to drop back that season into the basement division from whence they had come only two years earlier. They were cannon fodder for any club with designs on a good run - something Albion most certainly had following their dominance of the League Cup in the previous two seasons.

But the First Division side were entitled to harbour a few feelings of anxiety as their number came out of that famous velvet bag on Monday, January 8. And not just because of Colchester's proud boast that they had never lost at home to a First Division club in the FA Cup or League Cup and had been seen as serial giant-killers ever since Huddersfield had been slain at Layer Road in 1948.

Considering Newcastle and Fulham had been among their previous visitors and that Arsenal were given a major shock when held to a 2-2 draw in 1959 before making no mistake in front of 63,000 in the replay at Highbury, it was a proud record to carry into their first-ever meeting with Albion.

It wasn't that Alan Ashman's side were out of form or struggling for results. Nothing could have been further from the truth. Although beaten 4-1 at Liverpool only two days before the draw, they had been the talk of the country as they produced a tremendous festive double over title-chasing Manchester City. The two games pulled in more than 90,000 fans in total, left them fifth in the table and earmarked them as one of the teams of the season.

No-one doubted the peaks they could reach. In the autumn, they beat Leeds 2-0 at home, then crushed Burnley 8-1 before adding Tottenham's scalp with another two-goal success. Audiences further afield saw them win back-to-back games in mid-December at West Ham and Chelsea, the latter 3-0, so they were in good nick when the Cup came round.

But they had a nagging worry in the countdown. And it was all because they were also inclined to plumb the depths. Early in a top-flight campaign that was rattling along nicely under new manager Ashman, they had suffered another of the blips which gave the sceptics every justification for viewing the third-round tie as an accident waiting to happen.

John Osborne is left grounded in Albion's first game of 1968 as Geoff Strong heads one of the goals with which Liverpool beat them 4-1 at Anfield. Also in shot are John Talbut (left) and Doug Fraser. Picture courtesy of Liverpool Post & Echo.

In between drawing 0-0 at Stoke and beating Nottingham Forest 2-1 at home, Albion travelled to Third Division Reading in the second round of the League Cup. It seemed a banker away win for a side who had lost at Wembley in the competition only six months earlier and won a thrilling two-leg final against West Ham the winter before that. They lost 3-1.

The First Division big guns had allowed themselves to be hustled out of their stride by a hyped-up lower-division team at a cramped little ground. They had fallen flat on their faces in just the sort of challenge now awaiting them at Colchester's tiny Layer Road headquarters.

It wasn't a one-off either. Every bit as embarrassingly, Albion had lost 3-0 at Second Division Bolton at the third-round stage of the 1965-66 FA Cup. Then there was that almighty gaffe when, in the final weeks of Jimmy Hagan's management in March, 1967, they had snatched disgrace from the jaws of glory by turning a 2-0 half-time lead against QPR into a 3-2 defeat in the League Cup Final.

It was confirmation that Albion and Third Division opposition formed a cocktail with a devilish kick; a kick that usually landed in the pit of blue and white striped stomachs. So a trip to the garrison town of Colchester was nothing to feel too confident about.

Supporters were infuriated at how their side could raise hopes by playing out of their skin against glamorous opposition one week and then be made to look second best by also-rans the next. Did it take the big stage to turn them on? Were they repeatedly guilty of complacency when the challenge was more earthy? Or, amid their undoubted individual and collective talents, did a lack of mental strength keep bringing them down?

It was accepted that Albion fell short of what it took to seriously join the race for the League title. Fans had been weaned, though, on thrilling cup runs and those aberrations against Bolton, QPR and Reading were hard to take. They were also hard to forget as one-time chicken farmer Alan Ashman prepared to lead them into FA Cup battle for the first time.

The then four-time Cup winners had been starved of success in the competition in the 1960s. They had crashed 3-1 at Lincoln in the third round in 1960-61, gone out in round five at home to Tottenham in 1961-62 and succumbed to Nottingham Forest and Arsenal in the fourth round the following two seasons. Two successive first-hurdle exits followed and, even when Albion made it past Northampton in the third round in 1966-67, they were humiliated to the tune of 5-0 at Leeds next time out.

It wasn't an encouraging record to carry back into the FA Cup mixer as Colchester looked to add a big-name scalp to that of Third Division high-fliers Torquay from earlier in the competition. Similar Albion seasons of top-flight respectability had failed to bring success in the competition, so was this one really going to be any different?

It was ironic that, while the visitors and warm favourites were managed by a relative unknown in Alan Ashman, the minnows of Colchester should have at their helm a man known all over the football world. Neil Franklin had been an imperious centre-half with Stoke and, no fewer than 27 times, for England before turning his back on the domestic game and sensationally defecting to Bogota in search of big money just before the 1950 World Cup finals.

Colchester may have been a backwater but at least it was a possible route to bigger things. By heading to South America and the capital of Colombia, though, Franklin entered a cul-de-sac. He had moved to a country outside the jurisdiction of FIFA and, when the promised pot of gold failed to materialise, he was ostracised, his playing career virtually ended.

Come January 27, 1968, Franklin wasn't the only exiled Midlander lying in wait, hoping to pull off a spectacular ambush. Colchester skipper and right-half Derek Trevis knew all about Albion from his time as a player at Aston Villa, where winger John Martin had also seen service. From across the city came ex-Birmingham inside forward Peter Bullock and in goal was 19-year-old Ernie Adams, who was close to an England under-23 call-up.

But the sum of the honest individual parts was still hardly sufficient to trouble a Division One side. Or so it was assumed by all and sundry.....

During a countdown in which Albion sold their allocation of 4,000 tickets - six shillings (30p) for the terraces and ten shillings or seven and six (50p or 37p) for seats - there was a big-name managerial casualty elsewhere, the Hawthorns' 1954 FA Cup-winning boss Vic Buckingham being sacked by Fulham and replaced by another former Baggies favourite, Bobby Robson.

Albion's manager of the day took no chances in the build-up. He whisked his team away from the Black Country on the Thursday and opted for the seaside town of Clacton - a dozen miles or so past Colchester - as a suitable base at which to complete the preparations.

Ashman was happy that he had all personnel contingencies covered as well. He had had the luxury of being able to name the same 11 for the previous eight matches, the last of them a 3-2 defeat at Nottingham Forest, and hadn't made a single change since including right-winger Nick Krzywicki in place of Kenny Stephens for the 2-1 December 2 defeat at Manchester United.

The other ten positions had remained constant for a dozen games and, in many cases, a lot more. To offset any late problems, though, Ashman took Graham Lovett and Ian Collard along to contest the place on the bench in the days when only one substitute was allowed.

What Albion's players didn't have, except for painful defeats in face-to-face League Cup combat, was much experience of Third Division football, although Jeff Astle had played at that level for Notts County and had, by coincidence, scored the first of his 168 League goals (31 for the Magpies) in a 2-2 draw at Colchester early in 1962-63.

It wasn't just Albion's alarming vulnerability against lower-division clubs that made their pre-competition odds of 12-1 - one of the shortest prices in the field - a surprise. Even apart from their latest giant-killing humiliation at Reading, their away form had been patchy, with the concession of four goals at Southampton and Coventry as well as Liverpool.

On the other side of the coin, they had won away to Fulham as well as Chelsea, West Ham and the Manchester City side who were to go on and win the Championship the following spring.

Colchester had lost 2-0 at Bury the previous weekend - their third successive League defeat after suffering a Christmas double at the hands of Mansfield - but that didn't stop manager Franklin beating the drum after watching Albion in their defeat at Forest and praising their 'attractive' play.

"We believe in attacking football," he said. "I have always believed in it. We shall adopt the same policy against Albion. For us to try to keep out such an attack for the entire game would be almost like committing suicide. Our plan will be quite simple: To try to start with a burst and score an early goal.

"If we can do that, we might have them on the run. I know how First Division players feel when they are away to a Third Division team in the FA Cup. There's the sense of being on a hiding to nothing. The cramped ground and the feeling that the crowd are right on top of you are unfamiliar."

A forecast in the Birmingham-based Evening Mail the night before had Albion to win 4-0 and Franklin added: "We are realistic about our chances but the lads will go out to enjoy themselves. They have to fancy their chances just a little bit. As for the fans, the whole place is agog with excitement."

Unfortunately, the anticipation came accompanied by an outbreak of crowd trouble. There was fighting behind one of the goals before kick-off and police ejected six spectators. One youth suffered a head injury, an elderly man was knocked to the ground and the disturbance was deemed serious enough for Alan Ashman, chairman Jim Gaunt and secretary Alan Everiss to appeal for order.

Layer Road, where 8,000 fans had queued for tickets the previous weekend on a non match-day despite a normal attendance figure of around 4,000, was bulging at the seams with a crowd of 15,981 - only a couple of dozen short of its official capacity. Some over-enthusiastic watchers perched dangerously on the stand roof and there was a certain lion's den feel to it all.

Veteran locals took great delight in pointing out that it was 20 years ago to the day that Colchester, then a non-League outfit, had famously ousted a Huddersfield side who belonged among the country's elite at that time. And Albion, like the Yorkshiremen, were having to change for the day from blue and white stripes to red. The omens were not good!

If Albion didn't know it already, they discovered they were in a real scrap as Colchester's seven-goal leading scorer Reg Stratton bulleted a header over the bar from John Martin's centre. And the ground erupted in only the eighth minute when John Osborne, baulked by team-mate John Talbut, failed to deal with a Martin cross and left Stratton to head into an empty net.

Neil Franklin's plan had worked a treat and it looked a sure case of here we go again for jittery opponents who could easily have conceded another as the underdogs continued to snap away at them. Albion just couldn't get going and should have been further adrift when Martin crossed yet again and Stratton this time struck the underside of the bar with a header.

Although Tony Brown set up a chance that Clive Clark overran into Adams's hands and Brown then saw a well-struck show gathered by the keeper at his near post, they were rare moments of respite. The force was still very much with Colchester.

Martin got himself on to the other end of a centre as the barrage continued and his header flashed narrowly wide with Osborne struggling. The same fate befell Jeff Astle when he nodded over the bar and Nick Krzywicki's disallowed

A rare moment of promise from Albion at Layer Road as Nicky Krzywicki shoots wide of the near post. The winger was taken off at half-time.

goal for a foul on Adams following Clark's pass hinted that the favourites were getting a tentative foothold in the tie.

Even so, it was something of a bonus when the equaliser came seven minutes before the interval. Astle, having been denied by a tremendous save from a fierce drive to John Kaye's pass, was needlessly pushled in the area by Duncan Forbes, leaving Tony Brown to send the keeper one way and the ball just left of centre as he blasted in the first of his five successful FA Cup penalties.

Forbes, who was to score an own goal at The Hawthorns to help Albion to a 3-0 FA Cup third-round win over Norwich the following year, then cleared off the line from Krzywicki's shot before Bobby Hope twice went close. And there were appeals for a second penalty as Clark was bundled over.

Albion's performance was unconvincing to say the very least; many would say poor. They improved slightly in the second half but had another scare when Price was only just wide with a shot from a narrow angle. Then, in the very last minute, came an incident that has become part of Hawthorns folklore, Albion's heads slumping as sub Peter Bullock fired home what for all the world seemed to be the winner after Trevis had hit the bar.

It looked a good goal and John Talbut, thinking the Cup dream was over for another year, picked the ball out of the net and booted it out of the ground in disgust. As road-users ducked out of the flight path, so Albion realised the referee was reprieving them. He had spotted an infringement, disallowed the goal and returned the visitors' faces to something like a normal shade.

To this day, nobody knows why a free-kick was given rather than a signal to restart the game from the centre spot and Talbut still says of his first FA Cup game for the club: "We were ready to take up our positions for the kick-off and I was convinced our run had ended there and then against a Third Division side. It has remained a mystery to me for 35 years why that goal was ruled out.

"I thought it was fair. I've got no idea why the referee disallowed it. I don't think anyone asked him but there were something like 21 bodies in the penalty area and maybe he thought he had spotted a push. What I do remember is that there was no argument and no discussion with the linesman. He disallowed it for something he'd seen and we restarted, relieved to have a second chance."

Although Albion were edgy throughout, Tony Brown had no fears about taking the equalising penalty. It was the second of his record 27 goals for the club in the competition and he says: "I couldn't grab the ball quickly enough. Bobby Cram used to blast his kicks and, when I took over, I aimed to thump them straight down the middle, although I had placed them in the third team.

"I was lucky enough to develop a good strike of the ball and worked on the assumption that they would always go in unless the keeper got something solid on them. I can't understand players who don't like taking penalties. Goalscorers must back themselves from 12 yards with no-one challenging. At Colchester, though, we were just glad to survive because it was a right struggle."

All the post-match talk in the visitors' dressing-room was of the big helping hand from the officials. England's World Cup Final victory in 1966 made a balding Russian linesman named Tofik Bakhramov famous. Now, FA Cup third-round day two years later had elevated Ormskirk referee Arthur Jones to something like hero status in West Bromwich.

The feeling of relief was still evident on the coach outside the ground as the first hand of shoot was being dealt among the card school of Jeff Astle, Tony Brown, Doug Fraser, Bobby Hope and journalist Ray Matts. That was when winger Clive Clark stepped aboard and said what everyone was thinking: "Our bloody name's on the Cup if we can get away with a decision like that."

It was probably a sentiment that has been uttered among a thousand different sets of team-mates following escapes on third-round day. But the overriding mood on the winding roads of Essex was that the cards might just be stacked in Albion's favour. They had played dreadfully, yet they were still in the Cup and determined to cash in on their good fortune.

Third Round Replay

Wednesday, January 31

ALBION 4
Kaye 10
Astle 17, 30
Clark 80
COLCHESTER 0

ALBION	V	COLCHESTER
Rick Sheppard	1	Ernie Adams
Eddie Colquhoun	2	Dennis Mochan
Graham Williams	3	Brian Hall
Tony Brown	4	Derek Trevis
John Talbut	5	Duncan Forbes
Doug Fraser	6	Bobby Blackwood
Graham Lovett	7	Terry Price
John Kaye	8	John Mansfield
Jeff Astle	9	Reg Stratton
Bobby Hope	10	Peter Bullock
Clive Clark	11	John Martin
Nick Krzywicki	12	Brian Loughton

Attendance: 38,448
Ref: A Jones (Ormskirk)

Easy Does It

FA Cup replays came round much quicker in 1968. There was no insistence on a ten-day notice period to stage second games, so, if you drew on the Saturday, you tried again on the following Tuesday or Wednesday. And the draw for the next round was always on the Monday lunchtime in between.

Albion had not been handed a home tie by the men in suits at the FA for three years but, as they contemplated how to make sure they encountered no more alarms against Colchester, that sequence of misfortune came to an end. Alan Ashman's men heard on the radio that they had been given the incentive of a visit from Southampton or Newport in round four.

The South Wales club had pulled off an unlikely 1-1 draw at The Dell at a time when they still had another 20-odd years of Football League existence stretching ahead of them. In further echoes of the past, Southport faced 1966 Cup winners Everton on the original third-round day at Haig Avenue and lost 1-0 while Barrow acquitted themselves well in going down by the odd goal to Leicester at faraway Holker Street.

Elsewhere, there were big-name casualties. Newcastle, three-times FA Cup winners in the 1950s, were beaten by visiting Carlisle (managed until a few months earlier by Alan Ashman) and Wolves went out at Tommy Docherty's Rotherham, a club rooted at the foot of the Second Division.

Arsenal needed two goes to oust Shrewsbury, Liverpool likewise against Bournemouth and League champions Manchester United were edged out by the only goal of a replay with FA Cup holders Tottenham. In the other half of Manchester, City thrashed Albion's League Cup conquerors Reading 7-0.

Alan Ashman needed no reminding about how close Albion had gone to another painful early exit. "Colchester played well and took advantage of being at home," he said. "We didn't play well. It's as simple as that. I think there's something in the possibility that our players had sub-conscious thoughts about the League Cup defeats against QPR and Reading."

At Layer Road, Ashman had replaced the ineffective Nick Krzywicki at half-time and so made Graham Lovett Albion's first-ever used substitute in the FA Cup. Lovett had also been the first sub thrown on by the club in a League match (at Northampton in September, 1965) and was destined to become their first sub in a European tie when he replaced Jeff Astle in the Cup Winners Cup clash away to Bruges in September, 1968.

Ashman had a three-way choice for the right-wing role for the replay, with Kenny Stephens also pushing for inclusion after being dropped nine matches earlier. In the end, he opted to hand Lovett a first start since his recovery from a serious neck injury sustained in a car crash 12 months earlier.

After all the stability of the mid-season months, a second change was forced when John Osborne, having made his FA Cup debut for the club four days earlier, failed a fitness test on a shoulder injury. Rick Sheppard took over - his first senior start since a 2-0 League defeat at home to Liverpool on September 2 and his first cup-tie since he was swamped during the 5-0 slaughter at Leeds the previous February.

There was also a doubt over Eddie Colquhoun because of a leg injury. But there was a boost for his club and his country when he was passed fit before kick-off. He had just been named in the full-back department in the Scottish under-23 squad for the game against England at Hampden Park the following midweek.

Come match night at The Hawthorns, Albion knew who they would be playing if they reached round four. Newport lost 3-2 at home to Southampton the previous evening. But Colchester manager Neil Franklin was sounding a familiar battle cry. "We will attack and we are just as optimistic as we were on Saturday," he said.

"I see no reason why we should have a change of heart. We know we should have won at home and Albion know they were lucky to get this second chance. The thing that holds back so many Third and Fourth Division clubs is that they go into ties like this feeling they are facing world-beaters. With the way that we worried Albion on Saturday, we have shown that definitely isn't the case with them and us."

Unlike in the first meeting, Colchester were nothing like good enough to carry out their manager's instructions despite some uncertain early handling in the rain from Rick Sheppard. Albion's first home game in five matches in the

Jeff Astle, in pain from old boots, sticks out his right foot and scores one of his two goals in the one-sided third-round replay win over Colchester.

39

competition was utterly straightforward and the remarkable near-40,000 crowd witnessed a one-sided contest.

The hosts again played in all red, with Colchester once more changing from blue and white to amber and black, and needed only ten minutes to go in front. By the half-hour mark, it was all over. A fine run and 25-yard screamer from John Kaye was followed by a brace from Jeff Astle, both set up by Bobby Hope and the latter after the scorer held off Brian Hall to beat Ernie Adams from close range. Clive Clark rounded the slaughter off when he sidefooted in the fourth from Hope's cross ten minutes from time.

Referee Arthur Jones was again well to the fore. As a 'thank-you' for the gift he made to Albion in the first game, he was brought to his knees when winded by a Hope pass. Then, to add insult and embarrassment to injury, he was bundled over in a collision with Colchester's Peter Bullock. The crowd showed their sympathy in time-honoured fashion......

While there was good humour off the field, superstition played a part on it after Astle's failure to find the net in four games since Boxing Day. He changed his boots and resorted to an old pair for the evening in the hope of a change of luck. But he was so uncomfortable in them that he switched back at half-time AFTER striking twice to break his 1968 duck!

Graham Lovett, who was no more than a limited success as a right-winger, almost made it five and said afterwards: "It's great to be back in the first 11. I was satisfied with the way things turned out. I felt confident on the ball and, more importantly, I didn't take any knocks."

There was no reply from Colchester; not even much sign of one, although John Mansfield volleyed narrowly over. Albion took their foot off the gas and even had some criticism from their fans for doing so. There were tedious spells but it was a highly convincing victory, marked by a man-of-the-match midfield performance from Hope.

Astle's poor weekend showing was forgiven and forgotten despite Duncan Forbes's rugged attention. The first game at Colchester had provided an almighty scare but the replay was a case of job done efficiently, the outcome obvious in double-quick time. The 4-0 Evening Mail forecast was right after all - in a roundabout way!

For Graham Williams, progress was something of as relief. The skipper had lived through the giant-killings of the previous few years and had painful memories of the FA Cup as a whole. "I cried my eyes out when we lost in the competition at Lincoln in the early 1960s and again when we were knocked out at Leicester a few years earlier," he said.

"We were vulnerable against lower-division teams and thought we had lost it at Colchester. We were convinced the game down there had got away from us and were arguing among ourselves as we got ready to kick off again. Then, we realised the referee had seen something amiss and given us a second chance. Thankfully, there were no slips at The Hawthorns and we were on our way."

Now it was time to think about tackling Southampton on a fourth-round day which was sure to account for at least four top-flight clubs, Manchester City having drawn Leicester, Leeds been paired with Nottingham Forest, and Stoke emerge from the hat alongside West Ham.

Albion's tie was the fourth all-First Division clash and marked the first FA Cup meeting of the clubs since 1900, when the Saints had gone marching in with a 2-1 third-round win at The Dell against a team containing veteran keeper Joe Reader, experienced full-back Amos Adams and a once-capped England international half-back called Harry Hadley.

Sixty-eight years on, Southampton believed they were capable of a repeat result. They were awkward rather than formidable opponents but they had the feeling they could sink Albion's Wembley dreams while they were still in their infancy.

Fourth Round

ALBION 1
Brown 47
SOUTHAMPTON 1
Saul 44

ALBION V SOUTHAMPTON

ALBION		SOUTHAMPTON
Rick Sheppard	1	Eric Martin
Dennis Clarke	2	Dave Webb
Graham Williams	3	Ken Jones
Tony Brown	4	Hugh Fisher
John Talbut	5	David Walker
Doug Fraser	6	Jimmy Gabriel
Nick Krzywicki	7	Mike Channon
John Kaye	8	Frank Saul
Jeff Astle	9	Ron Davies
Bobby Hope	10	Terry Paine
Clive Clark	11	John Sydenham
Ian Collard	12	Denis Hollywood

Attendance: 29,957
Ref: R Paine (Hounslow)

Another Struggle

Southampton were something of a bogey side to Albion - and were to continue to be after their 1967-68 meetings. Although they had taken only one point out of four during tense games between the two relegation-threatened clubs the previous Easter, the Saints followed up with a 4-0 early-season win at The Dell and then forced a dull pre-Christmas 0-0 draw at The Hawthorns.

They had by far the worst defensive record in the First Division (61 goals against) and had sold Martin Chivers to Tottenham in January, 1968, for what was described as the 'mammoth' fee of £125,000, an English record. But they were always seen by Albion as a tough nut to crack.

Ted Bates, a distinguished former Southampton player who went on to become the Football League's longest-serving boss, knew he had a talented understudy for Chivers in Mike Channon. He also had an already established target-man and goalscorer in his £55,000 record signing from Norwich, Ron Davies, a man who played 29 times for Wales.

The Saints' season had not been unlike that of their fourth-round hosts. They were also prone to form swings, following up a 3-0 opening-day defeat at Newcastle with a thrilling 3-2 win against Manchester City and, also at The Dell, that 4-0 romp against Albion.

An extraordinary 6-2 victory at Chelsea at the start of September underlined what they were capable of but they showed the flip side of their make-up when beaten 5-1 at home by Leicester a month and a half later, a young Peter Shilton embarrassing his opposite number Campbell Forsyth by scoring direct from a wind-assisted drop-kick.

Forsyth lost his place to Eric Martin before the Cup came round and, although Jimmy Gabriel was beginning to find the defensive form that had made Bates so persistent in his efforts to sign him from Everton the previous summer, Albion seemed to be meeting them at a good time. The Saints had gone into another nosedive by suffering five successive League defeats around the turn of the year and their struggle against a Newport side from the middle of the basement division was another embarrassment.

Even so, Albion had hardly sparkled in the immediate aftermath of the Colchester ties. The club announced they would be following up mid-1960s trips to South America and New York by touring East Africa at the end of the season at the invitation of the British National Export Council. But their hopes of spreading their wings to play in European football in 1968-69 depended on them regaining some form.

Eric Martin punches clear under pressure from Jeff Astle in the first half of Albion's letdown at home to Southampton. Clive Clark is to the left and Dave Webb the defender on the right. Photo courtesy of the Birmingham Post & Mail.

They blew a home derby by losing 1-0 against a newly-promoted Coventry side previously without an away League win and then lost Kenny Stephens to a three-week suspension after a sending-off in the reserves against Stoke. The winger, who had gone on as sub for Graham Lovett as the Sky Blues became the first away team to win at The Hawthorns for five months, was also hit in the pocket with a £10 fine.

Seven days later, Albion had to be content with a 1-1 draw from a trip to relegation-bound Sheffield United, where Asa Hartford made the first of his astonishing 900-plus haul of appearances for his various clubs. Hartford, soon dubbed the new Bobby Hope because of his Scottish roots and midfield creativity, made Jeff Astle's goal but his day was marred by a last-minute equaliser by Colin Addison.

That wasn't the 17-year-old's only connection with the senior no 10, who had been given his League bow at home to Arsenal eight years earlier at the age of 16. Hope's father actually discovered Hartford as both players had played for the same schools team in the Glasgow suburb of Clydebank

Hartford, who had been playing in the third team the previous season, was back on the sidelines for the Southampton clash as manager Alan Ashman kept faith with Rick Sheppard despite John Osborne's return to fitness. Ironically, the stand-in keeper had had to prove his own fitness following a training-ground collision with Dennis Clarke that led to both players going to hospital.

Sheppard had a cut mouth and Clarke needed eight stitches in a head wound but still took over at right-back from Scot Eddie Colquhoun, who was out after hurting his right knee when playing for Scotland under-23s. Clarke's only previous first-team start that season had been in the League hiding at Southampton and he was set to form an all-new pairing down the right flank. With Graham Lovett's comeback continuing to be stop-start, Welsh under-23 international Nick Krzywicki was named on the wing, having played well in a midweek reserve game at Nottingham Forest.

Southampton were struggling in the bottom three in the League but picked up a useful point at Forest the previous weekend and manager Bates said: "We shall go to West Brom with a good deal of confidence, based on our two matches against them this season. So far, they haven't scored against us."

Apart from the blip against Coventry, Albion were strong at The Hawthorns, beating Nottingham Forest, Sheffield United, Leeds, Burnley, Tottenham and champions-elect Manchester City since their home campaign had started erratically with defeats against Chelsea, Liverpool and Arsenal wrapped around a 4-1 taming of newly-promoted Wolves.

It was a sound record - but the Cup tie soon became one to forget. As at Colchester, Albion were dismal in the first half, although Tony Brown put Krzywicki through on a surge which ran out of steam near goal as the covering John Sydenham got back. John Kaye shot wide from Clive Clark's pass but three Southampton corners in the space of two minutes turned the tide, Sheppard having to pull down David Webb's shot from one of them.

It was no surprise when inside-right Frank Saul fired the visitors ahead on the stroke of half-time. Clark fouled Sydenham and gave Terry Paine the chance to swing over a free-kick to the near post, where the in-form Saul beat Sheppard from three yards.

Fortunately, Albion's general malaise did not engulf Brown, who had hit a rich vein of scoring form by netting in successive games straight after Christmas home and away to Manchester City and then away to Liverpool. His touch stayed with him against the Saints, although luck was on his side when he equalised two minutes into the second half.

From a flick into space by Kaye, Brown made good ground before chancing his luck with his right foot from all of 25 yards. The shot was firm rather than fierce and seemed to be safely covered by the usually dependable Eric Martin. But it took a freak bounce off a divot in the Birmingham Road End goalmouth and somehow ended up in the net.

"I couldn't believe it when my shot went in," Brown admits. "It wasn't that well struck and the keeper just went down on one knee to save. But the ball must have hit something uneven in the area and flew in over his right shoulder. They say you need some luck in the Cup and we certainly had some with that goal - and with what had gone on at Colchester in the third round.

"We started to think we might be on to something good in the competition, although we hadn't played well. It's a big lift when you get breaks like that going your way and I remember how keen we all were to make the most of our good fortune."

As Albion went out in search of a winner, Krzywicki remained involved in their most threatening moments. He connected with a header that Martin did well to save at the foot of his post after Doug Fraser had stormed down the right to cross, then he struck the upright before the keeper recovered more of his stripes by falling on a Jeff Astle header.

Despite their improved efforts, Albion couldn't build on their gift by going on to win. But the equaliser that put Brown on the brink of double figures for 1967-68 and alongside Astle as the club's two-goal top scorer in that season's FA Cup, did at least give a second chance to an out-of-sorts side.

Not that Bates was perturbed by what the following Wednesday night may hold in store. He had no injury problems for the replay and said: "We feel confident about the tie. It went our way in the first half at West Brom and we now know practically everything there is to know about them."

Bobby Hope still ackowledges the awkwardness of the two games against Southampton. He rates Brian O'Neill as the toughest opponent he ever faced and, although the midfielder was then still at Burnley before moving to The Dell, there were other characters in the Saints ranks who could be relied upon to provide a hot welcome in Hampshire.

"We always found it difficult getting anything down at their place because it was a tight ground and they were a physical, hard-working side," he says. "Players like Jimmy Gabriel and Dennis Hollywood were difficult opponents and even the forwards like Ron Davies and Terry Paine never forgot to let you know they were around. We knew we had our work cut out at The Dell."

Albion had already dug their way out of two holes into which their FA Cup hopes had threatened to disappear in double-quick time. Now, on another long trip south, they faced a much tougher test. If they failed it, they would be staring at what had become their annual early exit from the competition.

Fourth Round Replay

Wednesday, February 21

SOUTHAMPTON 2
Saul 10
Fisher 53
ALBION 3
Astle 16, 89
Brown 28

SOUTHAMPTON V ALBION

Southampton		Albion
Eric Martin	1	John Osborne
Dave Webb	2	Dennis Clarke
Ken Jones	3	Graham Williams
Hugh Fisher	4	Ian Collard
David Walker	5	John Talbut
Jimmy Gabriel	6	Doug Fraser
Mike Channon	7	Tony Brown
Frank Saul	8	John Kaye
Ron Davies	9	Jeff Astle
Terry Paine	10	Bobby Hope
John Sydenham	11	Clive Clark
(for Channon,82) Dave Thompson	12	Graham Lovett (for Osborne, HT)

Attendance: 26,036
Ref: R Paine (Hounslow)

'Just Great, Albion!'

Alan Ashman's men were facing a second testing trip south in the competition after the undignified scramble at Colchester - and the subsequent Monday lunchtime draw threw up the possibility of a third. In an either-or pairing on both sides of the small 'v', the names of they and Southampton came out alongside those of Portsmouth and Bobby Robson's Fulham.

The fact that the latter two clubs had to play again on the same night that Albion and Southampton went head-to-head made for a dizzy time for the Hampshire public and football authorities. And, as if the plot wasn't intriguing enough for the locals, with the very real possibility of a Pompey v Saints clash in round five, another strand was quickly added to the plot.

Hawthorns backroom man Stuart Williams, who had given the Baggies 12 years and 246 games of loyal service as a full-back before playing a further 175-plus matches for Southampton, was upgraded before the trip to The Dell from youth and Intermediate League team coach to first-team trainer.

The title may be unused today but made him coach to the senior side as well as sponge-man in the days before specialist physios. And the Welshman, who played more full international games as an Albion player (33) than any other man in history, was to have his medical skills tested straightaway.

Williams, born in 1930 and the holder of 43 Welsh caps when he hung up his boots, was summoned to The Hawthorns in 1966 when Jimmy Hagan read in the Press of his retirement as a player with Southampton. As Alan Ashman's right-hand man, he was suddenly drafted in for this second Albion trip of the season to his former club.

In the same backroom reshuffle, Albert McPherson was downgraded from senior team duties and put in charge of the reserves while Jimmy Dunn - an FA Cup finalist with Wolves in 1949 - moved from second-team to youth commitments. It was a sign Albion's manager was not sitting on his laurels.

Three successive League defeats had persuaded him things could improve and Williams says: "I'd already had the privilege of working with some fine youth players at Albion like Asa Hartford, Len Cantello, Alistair Robertson, Jim Holton, Lyndon Hughes and Alan Merrick, as well as one or two more like Hughie Read and Hugh McLean who didn't quite make it. But I had no hesitation in stepping up when Alan asked me to.

"He had made it clear when he arrived at the club that he wasn't going to be bringing in any staff of his own and said he would judge us as he went along. Obviously, he and I hit it off because, during the weekend of the home tie

This platform for Southampton. From left: Ian Collard, Clive Clark, Graham Williams, Jim Gaunt (chairman), John Osborne, Dennis Clarke, Ron Potter, John Kaye, Alan Ashman, Graham Lovett, Bobby Hope, Stuart Williams, Doug Fraser, Tony Brown, Jeff Astle. Picture courtesy of Birmingham Post & Mail.

against Southampton, he called me to his house in Walsall and said he was planning to make an announcement about the changes. Then, on the Monday, he called all the coaches together and explained everything."

Ashman was also busy ringing the changes with his players' pre-game routine. Having taken them out of town for the night before the home clash with Southampton, he delayed departure for the replay until match-day - and opted to let the train take the strain.

Nick Krzywicki was left at home as the troublesome right-wing role passed to Tony Brown - highly effective as an attacking central midfielder - while John Talbut (eye) and John Kaye (leg) had recovered from weekend knocks and defender Eddie Colquhoun was also fit, although ultimately made to wait for a recall as Dennis Clarke was retained at right-back.

Two heads rolled after the flop in the original game. John Osborne replaced Rick Sheppard in goal while Krzywicki's exclusion brought Ian Collard into midfield for his first senior game since the 2-1 defeat at Everton on October 21. It being a long trip, Ashman took the precaution of adding Ron Potter - a centre-half and no relation to long-serving keeper Ray Potter - to his squad.

The players awoke on match-day to unwelcome news. The south coast had been hit by heavy rain and pools of water lay on the pitch. In Osborne's case, the day also dawned with a rap on the window from a clothes-line prop wielded by John Kaye. The keeper was accompanying Kaye and John Talbut to New Street railway station and had overslept.

When he came to his senses, he realised the weather had done Hawthorns hopes no favours at all. Although the game was expected to go ahead, the anticipated muddy conditions were certainly not seen as conducive to Albion's more refined passing style.

On their trips to Southampton, the club always used a hotel the players nicknamed The Dead Parrot. The tag had nothing to do with dodgy kitchen customs. The cooking was fine. It's just that the establishment's real name was The Polygon!

Little could the squad have known as they tucked into their pre-match meal what a highly eventful evening they were in for. The game was only ten minutes old when John Osborne was knocked out as Frank Saul raced on to a long through ball from Terry Paine and drove home the opener. It was a fourth goal in four FA Cup ties in 1967-68 for the forward, who had also scored in Tottenham's 2-1 win over Chelsea in the previous season's final.

The early breakthrough had damaging repercussions. Osborne was caught on the chin in the process and resumed in a dazed state following three minutes of treatment from the already-busy Stuart Williams. With Ron Davies having gone close with a header in only the second minute and seen Osborne clattered again, the omens were not good for Ashman's men. The crammed-in 26,036 crowd scented blood; Albion's.

But, amid the backroom swap and their New Year injury problems, the club had made one other important switch. Among the human cargo on that rail journey south, they had packed something that came to be seen as their loyal protector - their all-white change strip. The new colours were first seen at Stoke in 1964-65 and, in early 1968, became regarded as lucky.

The storm was weathered, Southampton's early fire burned itself out and Jeff Astle equalised in the 16th minute, finishing smartly from close range after fellow striker John Kaye had helped back Bobby Hope's cross. Only 12 minutes later, Tony Brown followed his pal to the three-goal mark for the Cup campaign when he slammed home a poor clearance by Jimmy Gabriel with keeper Eric Martin off his line after a cross by Graham Williams.

The damage could have been greater still for the Saints as shots from Brown, Hope and Ian Collard rained goalwards. But worries were building at the other end. Osborne, although well protected by the men in front of him and little troubled by Southampton shots, was still concussed and in such discomfort that Stuart Williams felt unable to leave him unattended. A change would have to be considered, although the decision was deferred until half-time.

"Ossie's vision was blurred to say the least and I recall going and standing by his post while the match was in progress," Williams said. "I was yelling instructions like: 'There's a cross coming over from the right, it's going to drop

The Saints try to press home on attack. Substitute goalkeeper Williams is punching the ball clear of Mike Channon and Ron Davies.

Saints' goalkeeper Eric Martin makes a save with Ken Jones guarding the far post.

This page and the next show how the Southampton evening newspaper, the Southern Evening Echo, covered a dramatic replay night at The Dell....

Saints out of the Cup

By "OBSERVER"

Saints 2, West Bromwich Albion 3

E Saints made an inglorious exit from the Cup at The Dell last night, and so missed the opportunity of a fifth round tussle with Portsmouth, who won their replay with [...]m.

Far their own replay the Saints had the advantage of [...]ing at home, and had beaten West Bromwich there [...]ier this season. They scored an early goal and then [...] their opponents deprived of their regular goalkeeper [...] injury. Yet it was West Bromwich who rose to the [...]sion to snatch victory with a last-minute goal.

[...]d. Bromwich were without [...] goalkeeper John Osborne for [...] whole of the second half. For [...]t of the first half he was in [...] [...] after collecting a blow [...] the chin as he tried to save the [...]s' first goal in the 10th [...]te. The injury was aggra- [...]d by another collision soon [...]wards, but Osborne played [...] with coach and trainer Stuart [...]nns (the former Saints [...]er) remaining near the goal [...] half time.

Forward, too, the Saints were [...]interesting, with only Saul and Davies ever really looking like goalscorers. There were too many that lacked punch.

Generally the Albion players were sharper, more accurate and more "on their toes" than the Saints, and I thought they deserved their win.

Teams:—

Southampton: Martin; Webb, Jones; Fisher, Walker, Gabriel; Clanton, Saul, Davies, Paine, Sydenham. Substitute: Thompson.

West Bromwich Albion: Osborne; Clarke, Williams; Collard, Talbut, Fraser; Brown, Kaye, Astle, Hope, Clark. Substitute: Lovett.

Referee: Mr. R. A. Paine (Hounslow).

Attendance: 26,036; receipts £7,413.

Prizes

Prizewinners in the Dell Supporters' competition at the match were: £25, M6775 (not claimed); ball, O1720 (not claimed); £2 prizes, F9720, K7594, K3920, M677, A265.

More Saints pictures appear in Page 12

[...] this time Osborne made [...]al clearances, but was not [...]bled unduly by the Saints who [...] have been expected to try [...] longe-range shots.

[...]hen rearranged the dressing [...]n in half time Osborne was in [...]dly comfussed state and could [...] resume. Shortly afterwards he [...] taken to hospital where he [...]ained all night. He was dis- [...]sed today.

Captain takes over

[...]ion captain, left-back Gra[...] Williams, took over in goal, [...]stitute Graham Lovett came on [...] inside-right and John Kaye [...]ed back into the defence.

[...]llains was beaten by Hugh

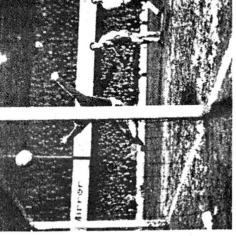

Hugh Fisher's goal which made the score 2—2 soon after half-time. Substitute goalkeeper Graham Williams makes a vain attempt to reach the rising ball.

POMPEY'S NIGHT TO REMEMBER

A "GOLDEN" goal from the right foot of Mike Trebilcock, the Cornishman who joined Portsmouth from Everton for £40,000 last month, gave Pompey a 1—0 victory over Fulham in last night's replay and took them into the fifth round of the cup for the first time for nine years. Their last fifth round tie was against Burnley in March, 1959.

It was a night to remember at Fratton Park with Portsmouth's enthusiasm eventually sweeping aside a nimble Fulham team although there were many anxious moments in the second half when Haynes and Co. came back into the game.

Only two brilliant saves by Milkins from headers by Clarke and Haynes maintained Portsmouth's lead and they now meet West Bromwich Albion in the next round.

The first half belonged to Portsmouth and Macedo was kept busy in the Fulham goal from the were a record for the ground even allowing for the £18 repaid to 80 spectators who demanded their money back because they could not see.

Pickpockets were busy. Seven wallets disappeared. One man had £40 stolen and altogether their haul was £90.

Teams—Portsmouth: Milkins; Tindall, Ley; Smith, Haydock, Harris; McCann, Pointer, Hiron, Kellard, Trebilcock. Sub: Travers.

Fulham: Macedo; Brown, Dempsey; Ryan, Callaghan, Conway; Haynes, Earle, Gilroy, Clarke, Barrett. Sub: Nichols.

52

on your six-yard line, now go and get it!' More often than not, he did and he played well. I took some stick from the Southampton fans because of my connections there but I had a reply or two for them as well. Even today, I have them telling me that giving instructions like that was out of order.

"I knew all the Southampton staff well and, at half-time, we got their medical man, Dr Ramsay, to look at the damage to Ossie. He insisted there was concussion. I said: "Don't give me that! You just want him off." But he was adamant that it would be dangerous to leave him on any longer, so we had to make emergency arrangements."

There were no substitute keepers in those days, so an outfield player had to go in goal. Ashman's choice rested between Tony Brown, who two and a half years later was to don the green jersey at half-time at Blackpool, and skipper Graham Williams, who had Frank Swift as his boyhood hero and who started his career at Rhyl's Emmanuel Secondary School as a keeper.

He was the smallest man on the pitch at The Dell, though, and, despite his side being 2-1 up, Osborne's departure from the fray was a decisive swing back in the Saints' favour in the greater scheme of things.

"It hadn't been very reassuring for the rest of us seeing Ossie struggling and having his movements programmed by Stuart," said Graham Williams. "But, when I was growing up, my sole ambition was to be a keeper and I read all the stories about Frank Swift that I could lay my hands on.

"I often still played as a keeper in training matches and I had kept goal in a reserve game when Clive Jackman was injured, so I suppose that's why I was chosen. But the changeover wasn't very smooth and it was a bit chaotic in the dressing-room before we went out again.

"Graham Lovett was sent on as substitute at the same time and perhaps Bomber Brown would have looked more the part in Ossie's gear than I did. I had a nightmare during the interval getting kitted out and my mind went back to when we were setting off once for a game at West Ham and Jimmy Hagan made sure I had my tracksuit bottoms packed in case our keeper was injured and I had to go in.

"Preparations were nothing like as professional as they are now and we didn't carry many spares. There certainly wasn't a second keeper's jersey in the skip that night. Ossie was 6ft 2in and I was 5ft 7in, so you can imagine what his jersey looked like on me - huge, especially round the shoulders. I also had his gloves on and they weren't a good fit either. Ron Davies, who, like Stuart Williams, was a team-mate of mine with Wales, was having a good laugh. Then he proceeded to give me a right pounding!

"Southampton had two good wingers in Terry Paine and John Sydenham, so big Ron, who was always a threat in the air, must have thought he was going to be in business. The crowd were wound up as well. They were always very close to the pitch at The Dell and I remember being hit on the back of the neck by a lot of cigarette butts.

"Maybe they were taking it out on me because of an incident earlier on. I didn't like Terry Paine and, thinking this would be one of my last trips there, I made it my business to clobber him. A high ball between us gave me my chance. Seeing a striped shirt out of the corner of my eye, I caught him a beauty in between the shoulders and he went down in agony. When I picked myself up, who should I see walking towards the scene of the incident but Terry Paine? By mistake, I had pole-axed Hugh Fisher, my old friend from Shropshire!"

Eight minutes after the interval, Fisher extracted revenge when his cross-shot from a corner flashed past the stand-in keeper for his first Saints goal and the scores were level at 2-2. Albion were down to ten men at the time, with Jeff Astle receiving treatment to a leg injury sustained when colliding with Martin. It was just one more cue for Stuart Williams to earn his money!

Things now looked decidedly grim for the visitors, who had John Kaye playing as an emergency defender and substitute Graham Lovett in the vacant inside-right role. Kaye linked up with John Talbut at centre-half and proved that an uphill struggle was just the sort of challenge to bring the best out of him.

It was just as well Astle returned to the fray. With only 60 seconds to go and 30 minutes of extra-time stretching uninvitingly ahead of Ashman's patched-up team, the striker knocked in a dramatic winner after Clive Clark had crossed back into the middle following Lovett's run and shot against the post.

Graham Williams wore a huge smile at the full-time whistle and spun on his heels as he used both hands to aim v-signs at the home supporters who had been goading him throughout the second half. Then his namesake praised him for performing between the posts 'as well as an established keeper.'

In the heat of the battle in front of him, Doug Fraser had one of his finest games for the club and Albion's dressing-room was an intoxicating place to be afterwards as photographers milled around to capture the happy faces of Graham Williams and Jeff Astle, in particular, for the following day's editions. One headline said simply: 'Albion, You Were Just Great!'

The players were in high spirits as they headed back to the 'Dead Parrot' for a meal. They were further cheered when they were able to watch the game again in the comfort of their hotel, a late-night TV show beaming highlights of a tie that truly ignited their stuttering FA Cup season.

There was a notable absentee during the celebrations on the train home. The collision with Frank Saul's boot had necessitated a trip to hospital for John Osborne, who was detained overnight for observation. "I don't remember a thing about the match, least of all my blow on the head," he said next day. "But it sounded really exciting when I read about it in the papers! I'm feeling okay now and obviously overjoyed with the win."

Manager Alan Ashman was concerned for the health of his keeper and said: "I had no idea how bad Ossie was until half-time. I tried to ask him then how he was and he just slumped in his seat. He didn't know where he was or what time it was and getting him off to hospital was the sensible thing to do."

The victory had been achieved in the face of massive adversity and was a wonderful start for Southampton stalwart Stuart Williams in his new duties. "We knew it was going to be difficult even with our strongest side out there," he added. "I was aware we had a decent bunch of players but I found out that night just how good they were, both ability-wise and in their attitude. They showed tremendous character and were obviously prepared to do anything for each other. It would have been easy to go out of the Cup there and then.

"I was just into my new job, so I couldn't claim much credit for the win. There weren't many secrets to facing Southampton. If you could stop Terry Paine, you cut off a lot of the supply to Ron Davies. The fact that Graham Williams was taken away from marking Terry in the second half made the win an even bigger achievement."

There were two interesting post-scripts to the dramatic tie. Defender David Webb didn't play another game for Southampton but his big FA Cup adventure was just beginning. He joined Chelsea a few days later and headed the winner for them in the replayed 1970 final against Leeds at Old Trafford. And the Saints covered his departure from The Dell by buying centre-half John McGrath.

Albion players always ribbed Jeff Astle that hard-man McGrath was one of the few opponents he didn't relish facing. The club's tough task over two dramatic fourth-round games, and particularly the replay at The Dell, might have been tougher still had the Mancunian, with his bulging biceps and legs like tree trunks, been signed a few weeks earlier.

That's TWO rounds we've gone through! Graham Williams' revenge at full-time.

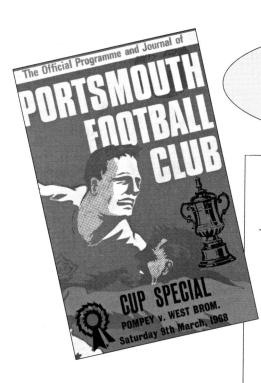

The Official Programme and Journal of...

PORTSMOUTH
FOOTBALL
CLUB

CUP SPECIAL
POMPEY v. WEST BROM.
Saturday 9th March, 1968

Fifth Round

Saturday, March 9

PORTSMOUTH 1
Hiron 75

ALBION 2
Astle 29
Clark 33

PORTSMOUTH V ALBION

PORTSMOUTH		ALBION
John Milkins	1	John Osborne
Roy Pack	2	Eddie Colquhoun
George Ley	3	Graham Williams
George Smith	4	Ian Collard
Ron Tindall	5	John Talbut
Harry Harris	6	Doug Fraser
Albert McCann	7	Tony Brown
Mike Trebilcock	8	John Kaye
Ray Hiron	9	Jeff Astle
Bobby Kellard	10	Bobby Hope
Nick Jennings	11	Clive Clark
Mike Travers	12	Graham Lovett

Attendance: 42,642
Ref: T Dawes (Norwich)

On An Even Keel

It was a case of two down, four to go for Alan Ashman's Albion and the omens were good as they prepared to follow up their successes over sides from the Third and First Divisions with one over Second Division Portsmouth in the fifth round. The signs could also be considered promising, though, for the high-fliers from Division Two.

Three times, the clubs had met in the competition and, on two of those occasions, the winners had gone on to lift the FA Cup, Albion prevailing in 1930-31 after a 1-0 success at Fratton Park at the same fifth-round stage and Pompey beating the visiting Baggies 2-0 in the fourth round in 1938-39 en route for a shock Wembley triumph over Wolves. Only in 1955-56, when Albion beat Portsmouth 2-0 at The Hawthorns in the fourth round, had a Cup clash of these clubs not preceded glory for the winners of their meeting.

In the 1967-68 tournament, Albion had already played four games - enough to have taken them through to the semi-final had they won their ties at the first time of asking and, in fact, the number of matches they had required to reach the last four in their last victorious Cup season of 1953-54. This time, four matches had been necessary to put them as far as round five, so the journey had already been something of a white-knuckle ride.

But the protracted ties - and the replays of contrasting difficulty - against Colchester and Southampton had not been without benefit. The eventual winning of them had contributed in no small way to the self-belief of a team who had shown themselves at The Dell to be masters in the role of underdogs.

No matter how much they struggled against Bolton, Reading, QPR or Colchester, they were a match for anyone on their day, especially if the chips were down. Cup progress, however torturous, had raised confidence levels.

Southampton's exit accompanied that of other fancied teams. Manchester City were also taken to a second game and weren't as fortunate as they went out 4-3 to Leicester. Stoke and Nottingham Forest were two other top-flight teams to bite the dust, against clubs from the same division, and Rotherham collected another good scalp with victory at Second Division Aston Villa. But there were no surprises at White Hart Lane, where Tottenham continued an ominous Cup defence by beating 1964 finalists Preston 3-1.

Albion may have conceded two at The Dell and one in the home meeting with Southampton but they were showing signs of becoming harder to beat. Three days after their arduous passage to the fifth round, they registered their first League victory of 1968 when Fulham were beaten at The Hawthorns. As at Craven Cottage in the autumn, Albion won 2-1 and the old firm of Astle and Brown came up with the goals.

It was a sign of increased defensive assurance that Stan Jones was allowed to leave on the first day of March. The Shropshire-born centre-half, a veteran of 267 Baggies appearances, including more than 100 in a row from 1962 to 1965, had been due to join Northampton the previous summer, only for a back complaint to scupper the move. But his return to fitness, coupled with the impressive form of his replacement John Talbut, persuaded Ashman to release him and he rejoined his former club Walsall.

As if to endorse their manager's judgement, Albion resisted soundly as they ground out a 0-0 draw in the League at Tottenham the following day. It was the fourth successive time they had prevented a side containing the hugely prolific Jimmy Greaves from scoring against them and the second season in a row they had left White Hart Lane with a goalless draw. At the heart of the resistance effort, Talbut marked English record signing Martin Chivers out of the game and was the star man.

The clash in North London, in which Bobby Hope, Doug Fraser and Eddie Colquhoun came under the gaze of Scottish international boss Bobby Brown, fell on a Friday night because of the League Cup Final the following day and Albion's players followed up an overnight stay in the capital by going to watch Leeds beat Arsenal 1-0 at the twin towers. It wasn't a good game and Jeff Astle was so unimpressed that he left the stadium at the interval and sat alone on the coach throughout the second half.

Ashman and his assistant Stuart Williams had the good fortune to miss the bore at Wembley, leaving themselves free to go spying on Albion's FA Cup fifth-round opponents Portsmouth. Their journey back to the south coast was for Pompey's Division Two home game against Birmingham - another side who were to become a subject of great interest to the duo a few weeks later.

Blues pulled off a surprise 2-1 win at Fratton Park thanks to defender Winston Foster's late header but the mission revealed little. Not because Williams was familiar with Pompey's players from his time at Southampton but because the second-in-the-table side who Albion were to face the following Saturday played poorly in their first home League defeat of the season.

Portsmouth's abrasive manager George Smith, a war-time Sergeant Major, had slashed his squad to only 15 and, although these were the days of only one substitute, he could accurately be described as running a tight ship in the football quarter of the naval city. Interestingly, he also had an informer in his midst in former Albion man Ray Potter.

The experienced keeper had not managed to dislodge John Milkins from the first-team picture after a Hawthorns career of 238 first-team games that included both legs of the 1965-66 League Cup Final triumph against West Ham. He was to turn out only three times in senior football for Pompey before his retirement in 1970 but he was ideally placed to offer extra insight into what made the likes of Fraser, Williams, Brown, Talbut, Kaye, Collard, Kaye, Astle, Hope and Clark - all long-time team-mates of his - tick.

Potter knew Milkins was in for a busy afternoon. Only twice in 12 games since Christmas had Albion failed to score and their League placing made a top-six finish a realistic aim. Even so, their front-line had to achieve a minor breakthrough to reach the quarter-final, Pompey keeping clean sheets both in the success over Fulham and their 1-0 third-round win at Peterborough.

Later in the Cup run, Albion's manager was to use getaway breaks as an essential part of the team's preparation, though you could have been forgiven for thinking he was averse to the idea judging by his comments before the Portsmouth tie. He quickly decreed there would be a normal week's training - for most of the week anyway - and decided against anything too different.

"It's no good organising special routines or rushing off to out-of-the-way places if you don't feel it will be of any benefit," he said. "These days, people are tending to move away from the so-called special Cup-tie training. I don't think my players would benefit from a change for a long period. The best way to keep the edge on their fitness is to stick with the normal routine as far as possible. We shall have a slight change in that we will set off on Thursday and stay for a couple of nights in Southsea. But most of our work will be done by then."

The 14-man squad contained no surprises. In addition to the 11 players on view against Spurs, Graham Lovett, Dennis Clarke and reserve keeper Rick Sheppard travelled, with John Kaye (after a stomach upset) and John Osborne (following sinusitis) returning towards full health with each passing day.

Portsmouth wasn't a totally new destination for Albion. They had pulled off a 1-0 win there thanks to a Jeff Astle goal in an ill-tempered friendly the previous summer but it was a step into the unknown for the vast majority of their supporters.

The clubs hadn't met in a League or Cup game since Pompey's relegation in 1958-59 when Vic Buckingham's Albion followed up a 2-1 September defeat at The Hawthorns with revenge only a week later to the crushing tune of 6-2 at Fratton, Ronnie Allen and Dave Burnside each scoring twice.

For the tie on March 9, 1968, a coach was even laid on for second and third-team players as the club had no other games that day. The motorway network being a skeleton of what it is today, fans started to leave as early as 6am, one operator alone laying on 25 coaches to a match for which Albion had been allocated 11,000 tickets and sold more than 8,000 of them.

Admission prices ranged from five shillings to ten shillings (25p to 50p) but the distribution itself didn't run smoothly with fans at one stage queuing for tickets that hadn't arrived. The club solved the thorny problem by taking names and addresses and then sending tickets out in the post.

The tie sparked even greater interest on the south coast. If Albion were excited about being in round five for the first time since 1960-61, Portsmouth (Cup runners-up in 1929 and 1934 as well as winners in the last season before the Second World War) were thrilled to bits at reaching the last 16. Not for nine years had they travelled so far.

On the same night that Albion's gutsy battlers had finally accounted for Southampton, Pompey edged somewhat fortunately past Fulham in a home replay thanks to a man with a famous FA Cup pedigree. Cornishman Mike Trebilcock (pronounced Tre-bil-co) was such a late emerger with Everton in their 1965-66 Cup run that he wasn't even named on the team list in the programme for the final against Sheffield Wednesday.

His answer to this oversight was to score twice in what was only his second Cup game, turn a 2-0 deficit into a 3-2 triumph and have his side's fans in such delirium that one of them ran across the hallowed acres with several policeman in pursuit while the match was in progress.

Against Fulham, Trebilcock struck with a right-foot winner in front of a crowd of 43,967 - the biggest at Fratton since 1952 when 44,699 had watched Newcastle's 4-2 sixth-round victory. The receipts were a club record £9,832, although £18 was repaid to 80 fans who complained because they couldn't see and pickpockets went to work to ensure that seven others went home poorer than they should have done.

Increased admission prices for the Albion tie meant the gate receipts record was raised once more, this time to £11,200, although the crowd figure was surprisingly down at 42,642. England manager Sir Alf Ramsey was among those present.

Pompey were without former England and Burnley forward Ray Pointer through a foot problem and made four changes to the side who had lost to Birmingham, one of them the welcome return to fitness of skipper Ron Tindall - also a prolific batsman with Surrey.

They represented an awkward hurdle for Albion but Ashman said: "We go there in confident mood. We will be out to repeat the form we showed at Southampton. That game did us a lot of good. The team showed character and played a lot of good stuff. We have generally been improving and teams are finding it difficult to score against us. Pompey didn't play very well against Blues and I suppose our trip to watch them was a waste of time for that reason. But their form for most of the season has been very good."

It was certainly a time for Ashman's skipper Graham Williams to exude confidence in the ranks. In the countdown to the tie at Fratton Park, he reflected on Leeds' victory over Arsenal in the League Cup Final and said: "Both teams were terrible - and they are supposed to be among the favourites for the FA Cup.

"We were lucky to get away with it at Colchester and we respect Portsmouth. There's no question of us going there and looking for a draw. We want to settle this one first time out. All the players are talking about Wembley and we think we can get there."

It was also a period when Williams demonstrated his versatility. A week after playing in goal at Southampton, he had lined up on the left wing in place of the absent Cliff Jones in Wales' 2-0 victory over Northern Ireland at Wrexham, where reported Albion target Ronnie Rees was among the scorers. Back with the club, the skipper - as Mr Organiser - had his team-mates' off-duty hours to help fill.

In the case of the stop-over at Southsea, that meant arranging a group trip to watch the newly-released 'Dirty Dozen' at a local cinema that was so small that some players had to go upstairs and some downstairs. Intimate would be an appropriate term to describe the setting, which was also a shade blue; especially when reserve keeper Rick Sheppard's colourful response to one of the more violent scenes echoed round the building.

The Friday night on the Hampshire coast also had a humorous spin-off for trainer Stuart Williams. Accompanying Ashman to the Southampton v Fulham First Division survival scrap, he found his way to the guests' car park barred and never did quite establish whether it had anything to do with Albion's triumph at The Dell two and a bit weeks earlier!

His mood was brightened the following day, but only after Portsmouth's eager start had been repelled. Right-back Roy Pack drove over the bar on the run, then John Osborne had to save at full stretch from Albert McCann following a short pass through the middle by manager's namesake George Smith. The keeper couldn't hang on first time but Graham Williams held off Ray Hiron's menacing advance.

Osborne then hurled himself bravely at the feet of Nicky Jennings as the winger cut in from his left flank, injuring his head in the process and needing treatment before resuming, and Pompey were looking much brighter than against Blues. They fired another warning shot, this time from Ley, and Albion's busy keeper was again tested.

As the first half progressed, though, so the class gap between a club striving to reach the First Division and one who had been in it for nearly two decades became apparent. Portsmouth were all endeavour and at times threatening but Albion's top-flight know-how told in the late-winter sun and the tie was settled

Doug Fraser leaps out of the way to avoid treading on John Osborne as the keeper grabs a loose ball in the first half at Fratton Park. Graham Williams (right) covers.

in a spell of little more than four minutes around the half-hour mark.

First, Jeff Astle, who scored many of his goals with superbly timed leaps at the far post, kept his feet on the ground but crucially lost his marker Harry Harris as he ran forward to meet Bobby Hope's chipped 29th minute free-kick from the right and steer a low header past the right hand of the motionless John Milkins - "a half chance superbly taken" as one newspaper put it.

Then, Eddie Colquhoun took the ball out of defence at the start of a move which saw Doug Fraser advance on to John Kaye's pass to find Clive Clark with a square pass that the winger drove in left-footed from inside the six-yard area with the help of a deflection.

The goals had come easily to Albion, who had gone close in only the second minute when Kaye was denied by a brilliant save from Milkins. They were near to adding to their lead through Astle and Clark, although Osborne threw himself high to his right to superbly fingertip away a Bobby Kellard header following McCann's centre.

Kaye, a defensive hero in emergency at Southampton, again dropped deeper after the break and, with Osborne and John Talbut in charge, and Williams outstanding, Pompey threatened only when left-winger Jennings chanced his luck from all of 25 yards and saw Osborne dive to clutch it two-handed.

HIRON SCORES

Pompey centre-forward Ray Hiron leaps to head the ball through the West Bromwich Albion defence to make the score 2—1.

And here's how the Portsmouth Evening News of March 11 portrayed Cup day in pictures....

Harry Harris (left), watches for a slip as a centre is taken from the air by Osborne.

Albion looked safe at one end and a handful at the other, Astle capitalising on another brilliant delivery from Hope to unleash a powerful cross-shot that Milkins pushed away. Clark quickly returned the ball to the danger area, where Astle this time saw a drive kicked off the line by Ley. The centre-forward still wasn't finished and was only just wide with a glancing header.

There was an unsavoury hold-up when Talbut went down after being struck on the head by a missile thrown from the packed crowd, a policeman already having walked on to the pitch at the covered end of Fratton Park to reprimand the defender for swearing in earshot of spectators.

Nevertheless, the tie was proceeding smoothly for Albion until, somewhat against the run of play, centre-forward Hiron headed home from close range after the unmarked Trebilcock had nodded a 75th minute right-wing corner by McCann back across the six-yard area from the far post.

Osborne then saved superbly from McCann and, in a late rally, the little

Bobby Hope looks on as Albion skipper Graham Williams sticks out a long left leg to keep Portsmouth's Ray Hiron at bay in a first half in which the visitors scored twice.

right-winger fired narrowly wide, leaving Albion grateful to hear Norwich ref Tommy Dawes' final whistle. "I sat there biting my nails," Ashman admitted. "Pompey's final assaults went close to snatching the win away from us."

Portsmouth boss George Smith praised his side's upping of the tempo and said afterwards: "We put up a great show in the second half. With less efficient goalkeeping, we might have drawn or even won." He had complimented Albion on their draw at Tottenham but was hardly gracious now in defeat, adding: "If they win the Cup, the competition will be devalued."

It was an uncalled-for slur and Jeff Astle was unable to restrain himself from having a go back. "If Portsmouth are in the running for promotion, there must be some pretty poor sides in the Second Division," he said. "If necessary, we could have scored one or two more. We fancy ourselves this season and think we can prove George Smith wrong."

The Portsmouth Evening News correspondent 'Linesman' was much more impressed and considered Albion a good side who deserved their place in the quarter-finals. "Their defence was strong and well organised, their whiplash counter-attacks often had Pompey in trouble and they had a match-winner in always-menacing centre-forward Jeff Astle," he wrote.

Victory at Fratton Park was the perfect antidote to supporters still numbed by years of FA Cup failure. Albion, again well served by their all white change strip, were two rounds from Wembley and in the last eight for the first time since, in the emotional aftermath of the Munich air crash, they had lost to a late Colin Webster goal in a sixth-round replay at Manchester United.

It wasn't just the fans who were starting to think big. On the long journey back from the south coast - Alan Ashman's men clocked up a lot of miles in that Cup run as well as plenty of playing minutes - the team stopped in the delightful Oxfordshire village of Woodstock for their evening meal. It was the cue for director Tom Silk to allow himself something of an indulgence.

"We ate at a place called The Bear and everyone was understandably upbeat," recalls Ray Matts, then Albion correspondent of the Express & Star. "I sat with the directors, the players at another table, and Tom ordered a bottle of Lanson champagne, which may be fairly commonplace now, but which seemed like the real business back then. I was young and well impressed!

"I've been fortunate enough to eat in some great restaurants over the years but had the best piece of roast beef that night that I've ever had. I can't recall much about the game after all these years but I can remember the meal and the feeling among Albion's directors that 1968 could be the club's big year."

The Plot Thickens

No Midlands club had won the FA Cup for eight years since Wolves' 1960 triumph in a poor final against Blackburn. But Albion weren't the only club trying to strike a blow for the region. Birmingham were still in the hat, too, following their improbable feat of holding Arsenal to a 1-1 draw at Highbury.

Furthermore, the presence of the two Sheffield clubs, plus fifth-round head-to-head opponents Leicester and Second Division strugglers Rotherham, who had drawn 1-1 at Millmoor, raised hopes that Alan Ashman's men may land themselves another winnable tie next time out.

Anticipation and optimism soared yet further when Albion's name was the first one out of that hat in the Monday lunchtime quarter-final draw: They had a home game and, instantly, there was now the chance, following the long trips to Colchester, Southampton and Portsmouth, that the club could conceivably win the FA Cup without having to play on another opponents' ground. Just as quickly as hopes rose, though, a blast of reality swept through the Hawthorns ranks with the words 'will play Tottenham Hotspur or Liverpool.'

Notwithstanding the fact they had home advantage, Albion had pulled out possibly the toughest nut of the lot. If they were going to lift the Cup, they were going to have to do it the hard way. Either they would have to knock out holders Spurs or bring down the 1964-65 winners and the 1965-66 Football League champions. A second visit to Wembley in the space of 15 months suddenly looked a bit further away.

Albion had a fancy that they could beat Tottenham - after all they had done so 2-0 that very season before hanging on for a late-winter goalless draw at White Hart Lane. By contrast, they had lost home and away to Liverpool, 2-0 and 4-1. The potential clash with Spurs not only appeared slightly easier. It also offered the better omens, along similar lines to the history between the Baggies and their latest victims Portsmouth.

Albion had seen the Londoners off 3-0 in a home quarter-final in 1953-54 and gone on to lift the Cup for the fourth time. Interestingly, Tottenham had then turned the tables with a 4-2 fifth-round win at The Hawthorns in 1961-62 - a season in which they had triumphed at Wembley.

So much for the signs in the stars! The truth was that Liverpool stood squarely in the path of both clubs and the smart money was on them going through at Anfield after emerging intact from their visit to the capital. The bookies were certainly in no doubt. The Merseysiders' odds of 5-1, compared with Albion's 9-1 and Spurs' 16-1, showed how big the latter duo's task was.

If Alan Ashman was disappointed, even daunted, by the pairings, he didn't show it as he made early plans to take in the Anfield replay. "It's a great draw," he enthused. Probably only he and his nearest and dearest knew if he meant it! The manager added: "At this stage, there are no easy sides. The best you can hope for is to be drawn at home and this has gone in our favour.

"We can't afford to leave anything to chance so we shall watch the Liverpool v Spurs game and watch the winners constantly until the sixth round. Having said that, we have played both teams home and away this season, so there is plenty we already know about them."

Albion also had the security of knowing they would definitely be part of the drama three weeks down the line. Six of the other teams, plus Liverpool and Tottenham, still had unfinished fifth-round business. Stan Cullis's Blues or Bertie Mee's Arsenal would be at home to Chelsea or Sheffield Wednesday, who had also finished all square, while Rotherham and Leicester had to meet at Filbert Street for the right to take on visiting Everton.

The only definite quarter-final tie was the all-Yorkshire showdown between Leeds and Sheffield United - no doubt a big factor in the bookies making Don Revie's team 9-4 favourites to lift the Cup. Everton were alongside their Merseyside neighbours at 5-1, Chelsea were 7-1, Leicester 10-1, Arsenal 16-1 and Birmingham a distant 25-1.

There wasn't much time for Albion to rest on their Cup laurels. They were back in First Division action at home to Stoke the following Wednesday, when Tony Brown was rested after playing at Portsmouth despite flu. He was joined on the sidelines by Bobby Hope and Clive Clark, who had picked up knee injuries at Fratton Park, the resulting changes adding more fuel to the debate over who might fill the troublesome right-wing role on a regular basis.

For the visit of a Stoke side just back from a mid-season jaunt to Ghana, Kenny Stephens was entrusted with the shirt while Graham Lovett returned at inside-left and Dennis Martin, a £5,000 buy from non-League Kettering, was handed his debut on the left. The switches were not a roaring success.

Albion won 3-0 but only thanks to three goals in the last 20 minutes of a performance of no great merit, Jeff Astle beating Gordon Banks with one of only three penalties in his club goal tally of 174. The evening had a further surreal feel to it with the visitors playing the first half in red and white stripes and the second in plain red shirts after the referee had, not surprisingly, deemed there to be a clash of colours.

With the on-field fare doing little to lift the crowd, there was almost as much interest in events elsewhere. Although the Liverpool v Spurs replay had been put back to the following Monday because of international games, this was the evening Chelsea overcame Sheffield Wednesday 2-0 at Stamford Bridge and

Leicester proved much too powerful for Rotherham at Filbert Street.

In a big eye-opener the previous evening, Birmingham bridged the gap in divisions by bringing down Arsenal 2-1 at St Andrew's thanks to two goals by Barry Bridges either side of one from Bobby Gould in a tie witnessed by Albion duo John Talbut and John Kaye.

And there was drama when Liverpool and Tottenham belatedly met. Roger Hunt's opener and Cliff Jones's 88th minute consolation were routine enough but, in between, Tommy Smith scored the killer second goal from a penalty that had to be retaken when it was discovered Spurs had 12 men on the pitch!

With the holders out, Albion were left with one Merseyside team on their minds as far as the FA Cup was concerned. But they had to focus their sights on the other when Everton headed for the Black Country with League points at stake a fortnight before quarter-final day. The transfer deadline had fallen the previous day and Ashman showed he was not prepared to let the grass grow under his feet by committing a club record £65,000 on Coventry's Ronnie Rees.

The winger, the subject of a failed Albion bid a few weeks earlier, had 12 Welsh caps and was to finish with 39 from a three-club career that also took in Nottingham Forest. If his Hawthorns debut was memorable, though, it was for all the wrong reasons and Ashman must have wondered whether he should have spent his money strengthening a defence he thought had finally been put right.

Everton ran riot. Two goals in three minutes by Alan Ball had them firmly in control by the middle of the first half and, although Ian Collard pulled one back before the interval, the lead was stretched to 6-1 before Collard netted again for what was a very scant consolation goal, Ball having taken his total for the day to four, including two penalties.

England manager Alf Ramsey witnessed the mayhem as Albion were made to suffer their highest goals-against tally in a home League match since 1937, when Sunderland came and conquered to the tune of 6-1. Kenny Stephens went off with a twisted knee in the first half and Rees later pulled a muscle but even these blows, on top of the absence of Brown, Hope and Clark, could not excuse how Albion's stout resistance over several weeks had crumbled alarmingly.

Everton had four teenagers in their side and midfield maestro Ball had been doubtful before the game. But the firebrand England World Cup hero played and scored what were to later emerge as some useful psychological points on a day when Joe Royle and John Morrissey were also on target.

The ITV cameras were present to increase Albion's embarrassment in extended highlight form the following afternoon and the rearguard who folded so disturbingly did little better at fellow Cup quarter-finalists Leicester seven days later. With Rick Sheppard given a rare outing in place of John Osborne, the side were two down with 16 minutes to go and on their way to a second successive confidence-lowering defeat. Then, a much-needed show of that famous Cup-fighting spirit was transferred on to the League stage.

Clive Clark, who had returned to action along with Bobby Hope and Tony Brown to the exclusion of Kenny Stephens, Graham Lovett and the unlucky Ian Collard, scored twice in quick succession from the left wing and, five minutes from the end, forced Peter Shilton into a parry that gave Jeff Astle the opportunity he took for an undeserved winner.

Albion had somehow extracted two points from a miserable performance and given themselves a tonic for the visit of mighty Liverpool the following weekend, even if they knew they could forget all about progressing in the Cup if they played as badly again. Furthermore, Clark's two goals at Filbert Street, and one at Portsmouth, confirmed he was back in form with a vengeance after a dip.

Off the field, Clark was something of a loner with some curious ways. His team-mates noticed his habit of regularly clearing his mouth of even the tiniest bits of spit and he once bought his wife a pet poodle 'Pele' that bit him on the nose. On the pitch, he was a terrific cutting edge in a hugely entertaining Albion side, described by Jeff Astle as 'a brilliant little winger who was afraid of no-one'. Quick, brave and tricky with a penchant for winning penalties, he would be worth millions today.

In five successive seasons from 1963-64, he scored ten or more, his best 1966-67, when he netted 29 times, including one in each round of the League Cup and two in the Final against his old club QPR.

He fell out with Jimmy Hagan in 1965 and was so fed up that he even talked about quitting football. But the rift was healed and he stayed for four more years that took in the great FA Cup adventure of 1967-68.

Clive 'Chippy' Clark, a left-winger with a rare scoring touch, heads goalwards at Tottenham in October, 1965.

69

Sixth Round

Saturday, March 30

ALBION 0

LIVERPOOL 0

ALBION	V	LIVERPOOL
John Osborne	1	Tommy Lawrence
Eddie Colquhoun	2	Chris Lawler
Graham Williams	3	Emlyn Hughes
Tony Brown	4	Ian Ross
John Talbut	5	Ron Yeats
Doug Fraser	6	Geoff Strong
Nick Krzywicki	7	Ian Callaghan
John Kaye	8	Roger Hunt
Jeff Astle	9	Alf Arrowsmith
Ian Collard	10	Ian St John
Clive Clark	11	Peter Thompson
(for Collard, 74) Kenny Stephens	12	Bobby Graham

Attendance: 43,503
Ref: J Carr (Sheffield)

A Tense Deadlock

Liverpool may have won the League Championship in both 1963-64 and 1965-66, the FA Cup in 1964-65 and finished runners-up in the 1965-66 European Cup Winners Cup. But there was an unmistakeable feeling that the Albion sides of the same era had the beating of them. And the reason for their optimism was down in the record books in black and white.

In 1965, they followed up an end-of-season 2-2 draw with the champions at The Hawthorns by thrashing them 3-0 on their next visit in the autumn. They then travelled north five and a half months later and had even the home fans chanting their name as they beat Bill Shankly's awesome side by the same scoreline on what proved a particularly rewarding night for John Kaye. He had taken a fancy at Sandwell Park to a set of golf clubs owned by Albion chairman Jim Gaunt, who told him that, if he scored at Anfield, they were his for free. He did and they were!

The win, coming a week and a half after skipper Graham Williams had gone to spy on Liverpool in their FA Cup semi-final win over Chelsea at Villa Park, was yet more evidence of the dangerous knack Albion had of being able to match and bring down the very best on their day.

They strengthened the unlikely hold they had on the side destined to be their 1967-68 FA Cup quarter-final opponents with a win (again 3-0) and draw in the next season's League meetings and were to triumph 1-0 at Anfield in the following 1966-67 campaign. But, amid those memorable Baggies conquests, there was an FA Cup meeting that left a less pleasant taste in the mouth.

Albion were stuck in a dismal run of League form when they were drawn at home to Liverpool in the third round of the 1964-65 competition. At the time, they were in the advanced stages of a First Division sequence of seven defeats and three draws from ten matches and were unable to stem the tide in a tie they lost 2-1. But the clash contained an incident that would have provided dream What Happened Next? footage.

Albion were again trailing when Liverpool skipper Ron Yeats picked the ball up in his own area after hearing a whistle. He assumed it was from referee Kevin Howley but a supporter on the Birmingham Road End terraces had been responsible and a spot-kick was awarded. There was great amusement among the home fans, whose anticipation turned to despair when right-back Bobby Cram, having converted his previous five penalties, dragged his shot wide.

Liverpool survived to win by the odd goal, to beat Leeds by the same score five rounds later at Wembley and to become FA Cup winners for the first time in history. "I would never have lived it down if we had gone out at The Hawthorns that day," Yeats said in 2002. "Thankfully, we won and I became the first Liverpool skipper ever to lift the Cup. But I hated going to West Brom because they were always a hard side to beat."

Yeats was about to find out once more what a handful Albion could be as preparations were stepped up following the amazing revival by Alan Ashman's side in their victory at Leicester - on the day 5,000 fans filled the Throstles Club car park to queue for five shilling (25p) terrace tickets. Business was more than brisk and one enterprising youngster waited for two hours and then promptly sold his ticket for 7s 6d (37p) at a 50 per cent profit.

On the field, Bobby Hope - the man Liverpool manager Bill Shankly openly admitted made Albion tick - was doubtful with the knee problem he had aggravated at Leicester, where Eddie Colquhoun had gone off with a calf injury and John Osborne had missed out altogether because of food poisoning. Although the keeper was sent home again on the Monday, he and Colquhoun had recovered sufficiently to take part in a full-scale midweek practice match at the club's Spring Road training ground.

They knew what they were up against. Both had played in the 4-1 defeat at Anfield on January 6, when Roger Hunt hit a hat-trick, the England World Cup Final hero going on several weeks later to write his name in history as Liverpool's all-time leading goalscorer. Just to underline the size of Albion's task, Shankly showed a characteristic disregard of modesty on the part of his players and called them the best club side in the world.

Of the tie, he said: "This match is not as tough as having to go to Tottenham in the last round. Albion are a very good side but we have beaten them home and away this season in the League when they were at full strength. Without Hope, they are only half a team. And it's nonsense to suggest we shall be playing for another draw. We are going to The Hawthorns to win."

The fuse was lit and Alan Ashman had an unwanted distraction in Cup week in the form of some club business to attend to when, for the second time, Dennis Clarke and Kenny Stephens submitted written transfer requests due to lack of first-team opportunities. The manager spoke to both and, as on the previous occasion, told them they couldn't go.

Ashman also had a doubt over Jeff Astle because of a bruised thigh while Liverpool had worries over striker Tony Hateley and defender Tommy Smith, both of whom had leg injuries that had ruled them out of the League win at Sheffield Wednesday a few days earlier. They were already without left-back Gerry Byrne, who was out for the season and being replaced by Emlyn Hughes - one of John Osborne's least favourite opponents.

The guessing game continued as Albion set off for the pre-tie hideaway of

Droitwich in Worcestershire. Ian Collard, who had played four successive
League games before making way for Hope by dropping down to substitute at
Filbert Street, was very much on stand-by to start against the club he could have
joined as a teenager while Kenny Stephens and Nicky Krzywicki were again
contesting the right-wing role; a position this time made available as new
signing Ronnie Rees was Cup-tied.

There was a good omen for the tie as a four-man Albion side containing Alan
Ashman, Doug Fraser, celebrity fan and motorbike favourite Jeff Smith and star
man John Osborne beat Nottingham Forest to win BBC TV's Quizball Trophy.
It was an honour the keeper and former grammar schoolboy cherished almost
as much anything he won on the pitch! But the match the masses were more
interested in was likely to take a lot more winning.

Smith and Hateley failed their fitness tests, the latter having scored four
against Walsall in the fourth-round replay at Anfield. His absence let in Alf
Arrowsmith, who had hit the winner in the First Division game at Wednesday
and who had netted four times against Derby on his FA Cup debut in 1963-64.
Albion were, as expected, without Hope but Astle passed a fitness test and
Krzywicki was chosen on the right wing ahead of Stephens, who was sub.

The home side did the early attacking as Astle demanded a fine save from
keeper Tommy Lawrence before Krzywicki's close-range shot was blocked by
Smith's stand-in Ian Ross. No 2 Eddie Colquhoun lined up as a central defender

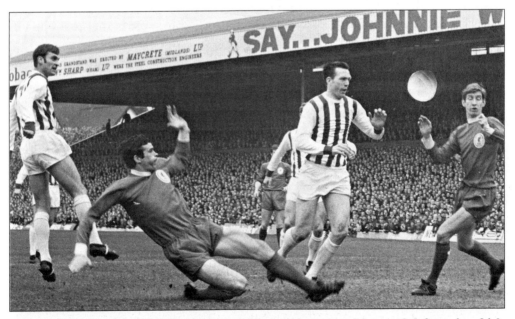

**Nick Krzywicki (left) and Jeff Astle cause big problems in a Liverpool defence in which
Ron Yeats is at full stretch as his team-mate Geoff Strong looks on. The Merseysiders held
out........for the time being. Picture courtesy of the Birmingham Post & Mail.**

to keep an eye on Roger Hunt while Doug Fraser played as a right-back in a defence who were relatively untroubled in the first half.

Most of the play continued to be in Liverpool's half and Collard was next to try his luck with a shot that flew wide from 20 yards after he had chested down a neat flick by Clive Clark. The midfielder did a tidy job in place of Hope and derived plenty of personal satisfaction as he gave further glimpses of the talent that had had Merseyside scouts homing in on him as a schoolboy due to the fact his teacher Rob Paisley was a nephew of Anfield legend Bob Paisley.

Liverpool were ordinary in the first half and Astle, just beaten to a through ball by Lawrence, was handed his chance when Clark quickly collected the keeper's clearance and whipped it back into the middle. The no 9 this time got in his shot, only to be denied by a diving save.

Shortly afterwards, Albion were out of luck when Tony Brown and Collard combined smartly on the half-way line to send the latter away for a dangerous cross that looked certain to set Krzywicki up for a telling shot. But Ross popped up from nowhere to produce a crucial challenge and block the effort.

And, shortly before the end of a first half dominated by the home side, Krzywicki got the better of Emlyn Hughes before delivering a centre that Yeats headed behind with Astle on his shoulder. The game had been as gruelling as expected and, in a prelude to what was to come later in the tie, John Kaye went off just before half-time for treatment to a facial injury.

Liverpool improved in the second half and might quickly have been in front when Ian St John sent Hunt away and his cut-in led to a cross that just eluded the stretching Arrowsmith. Then a mistake by Talbut, who hammered a clearance against Arrowsmith's knees, sent the stand-in centre-forward clear,

Alf Arrowsmith slides in on to a cross by Roger Hunt and just fails to make contact. John Talbut hits the deck as well. Picture courtesy of Liverpool Post & Echo.

only for him to delay his shot and allow Osborne to block with his knees.

Albion were now having to play more on the break and one counter-attack brought a disappointing lob by Krzywicki into Lawrence's hands after Brown had carved open the visitors' rearguard. Back came the Merseysiders, though, to go the closest to a breakthrough yet as Geoff Strong shot from 25 yards, had Osborne beaten all the way and saw the ball cannon out off the crossbar.

Stephens was thrown on in place of Collard for the final fling - but to no avail. Liverpool's mighty defence held firm and Albion's improving back-line, pierced no fewer than six times by the other big Merseyside club a fortnight earlier, did likewise. It was stalemate. On the day Red Alligator won the Grand National, the teams went the full distance and produced a photo-finish.

Albion hadn't been at their best, particularly going forward, but Alan Ashman wasn't too disappointed. He and his squad had been given yellow fever jabs three days before the tie in preparation for their end-of-season tour of East Africa and he had feared health repercussions, real or imagined.

Despite the cave-in against Everton, Albion were generally in a good groove and were in the middle of a run of five clean sheets in seven matches. Stuart Williams was priding himself on making the side harder to beat - a quality they would now need at Anfield - and had introduced what he considered to be changes for the better on the training ground.

"I was more worried about facing Liverpool at The Hawthorns than away," he reveals. "I just felt they could cause us more problems there and we were a shade fortunate to get away with a draw. But my reaction to facing a replay was: Right, we might have done the hard bit. Now let's go and beat them up there.

"In training, I had the players doing less running and more ball-work. Everything was geared to quick, sharp sessions. When I first said we were doing two-touch stuff in training, the players weren't happy. But, after a few weeks, they had really improved. And, when I asked them how they felt about going back to having more touches of the ball, they were against the idea.

"They had adapted really quickly and it wasn't only in the Cup that we did well. We hardly lost up to the end of the season in the League either. I only had to tell them once what we were doing in training and they would get on with it. They were absolutely fabulous to coach because they all had special skills yet they knitted together so well and carried that professionalism on to the pitch.

"I always thought the Welsh team I was lucky enough to be part of in the 1950s and 1960s was great in the way players mixed and welcomed newcomers in the right way. But I would put the atmosphere at Albion in the late 1960s in the same high category. They were special lads and I loved every one of them."

Williams was keen to dabble in the psychology of the game and made it his business to learn about the players' individual ways. "We are all different and I used to tell them I knew them better than they knew themselves," he added. "John Osborne would often be miserable first thing. He definitely wasn't a morning person. I would take the mickey, then make him feel special by saying what piece of training was being done with him in mind.

"Tony Brown was once going through a lean spell and told me he was worrying about it. I checked he had nothing preying on his mind other than not scoring, then told him the solution was easy: Just carry on doing exactly the same and the goals would come, which they did.

"Jeff Astle was at the other end of the scale to Alan Ashman. He was always noisy and the life and soul of the place day after day. He liked his food and a drink, so we had to keep an eye on his weight. On the dressing-room wall, I put up a sheet with what we decided was every player's optimum weight. If they went more than two pounds above it, their weight was recorded in red ink.

"This all became a subject of great banter when the players were weighed and all their team-mates would crowd round the scales for the reading. But it made everyone conscious of the need for self discipline because no-one wanted to be bantered about among their colleagues.

"Chippy Clark never put an ounce on but was a bit of a loner who would go for a wander and then reappear when we were getting on the coach or having a team meeting. Graham Lovett never had time to think about having a stroll. He was always arriving at the last minute anyway, especially when he was travelling into the ground on the bus.

"Ian Collard had a moan at me once, saying I never praised him when he had done well. My answer was that I was there to correct his faults. He didn't need as much time from me on his strong points. He lacked confidence and was self-critical, probably because he had to battle to win a regular place in the side."

Stuart Williams' confidence about the replay was echoed by the unrelated Graham Williams, for whom games against Liverpool usually meant a battle of wits and limbs with England World Cup 1966 squad man Ian Callaghan. But there was an edge, too, whenever he crossed paths with former Villa striker Tony Hateley, who was likely to be fit for the replay.

Williams had once been sent off in a victory at Aston Villa for an off-the-ball settling of scores with Jeff Astle's former Notts County team-mate and, as the players trudged wearily away from The Hawthorns on that quarter-final day, he set about scoring some psychological points. The tough-tackling captain pointed out Albion's earlier wins at Southampton and Portsmouth, and said to his rival: "That's you out now then, Tony."

The Ideal Incentive

It was 37 seasons since Albion and Birmingham had met in the FA Cup Final - a game won 2-1 by a Baggies side led by Tommy Glidden. And the possibility of another Throstles v Beau Brummie Wembley showdown was still alive on the Saturday night of quarter-final day, 1968.

Blues, superbly served at wing-half by Albion manager-to-be Ron Wylie, went through to the semis at the first time of asking as they followed up their lowering of Arsenal's colours by seeing off another of the capital's glamour clubs, Chelsea. The beaten 1967 finalists fell at St Andrew's to a 63rd minute header from Fred Pickering that proved the only goal of the game.

While fans around the Second City dreamt of a major May 18 exodus to Wembley, their counterparts 100 miles north could visualise an all-Merseyside final. Everton had finally conceded a goal in their Cup run when they took on Leicester at Filbert Street. But they scored three of their own and so added another scalp to those of Southport (1-0), Carlisle (2-0) and Tranmere (2-0). Compared with Albion's torturous Cup journey, Everton's progress was positively serene.

As millions of fans gathered round their wirelesses the following Monday lunchtime, Liverpool were 9-4 second favourites for the Cup. And the draw for the last four kept them apart from Everton, who were paired with favourites Leeds in a titanic semi-final. Leeds had beaten Everton home and away in the League that season without conceding a goal and their pairing meant there was still the chance of a second successive Liverpool v Leeds meeting at the twin towers.

Of much greater interest back in the West Midlands, though, was the potential mouth-watering collision between Albion and Blues. The two near neighbours wouldn't be meeting at Wembley but there was the opportunity for the next best thing if Alan Ashman's fighters could box their way out of their tightest corner yet.

The manager adopted a pragmatic view towards his team's Anfield replay assignment and knew the door to Wembley was ajar. The semi-final pairings also had a romantic undercurrent for the Midlands and guaranteed the region its first FA Cup finalist for eight years - the longest gap of the century at that point, war years excluded, between either Albion, Aston Villa, Wolves or Blues going to the last stage.

"We are still quietly confident," Ashman said. "It's ridiculous for anyone to say we have no chance at Anfield. That can never be the case when two Firs

Division clubs are up against each other. I do not regard our display in the Liverpool tie at The Hawthorns as a poor one and we could well have won.

"Clearly, we depend a lot on Bobby Hope. After all, there are very few players around of his ability. Now we have to try to get him fit as soon as possible and the draw is an extra incentive to us because Albion v Birmingham would be a storybook tie."

Skipper Graham Williams went a step further in expressing delight at the either-or pairing. "We did not

Bobby Hope at play with his team-mates on their trip to New York in the summer of 1966. As Albion prepared to step into the heat of Anfield, Bill Shankly reckoned they were only half a team without the brilliant midfielder.

fancy drawing Leeds, maybe because they had knocked us out 5-0 the year before and we had also lost there in the League the same season," he said. "We wanted to avoid Everton as well.

"Getting Blues in the semi-final was brilliant, even though we still had the small matter of Liverpool blocking our progress. A big cheer went up when we were paired with them. I used to live in Four Oaks, was friendly with some of the Blues players and well remember going out for a couple of meals with Ron Wylie, so that was another edge to the draw."

Birmingham manager Stan Cullis showed no reaction when the pairings came out. He didn't hear them. The former Wolves boss maintained his record of not listening to a single 1967-68 FA Cup draw as he kept an engagement at a Monday lunchtime Rotary Club function. It was some time later that he heard Albion might be next in opposition on the road to Wembley.

"There can be no easy draw at this stage but we must have a chance no matter who we end up playing out of Albion and Liverpool," he said later. And his quarter-final match-winner Fred Pickering was unashamedly bullish. "We would prefer to meet Albion but we also have the strength and skill to beat Liverpool," he said.

"On a personal note, it's fantastic for me to have got this far. When I was dropped for the 1966 FA Cup Final and sat on the trainer's bench to watch Everton beat Sheffield Wednesday, it was the greatest disappointment of my life. I thought my dream of a Final appearance had gone forever. Now, I'm only 90 minutes again from Wembley and my greatest wish is that Birmingham get through and our opponents are Everton."

Blues skipper Ron Wylie, who, like Barry Bridges and Bert Murray, had already been on the losing side in two FA Cup semi-finals, fancied a meeting with Albion but promised: "We would treat them with the same respect as we showed Arsenal and Chelsea. We have the greatest admiration for them."

The numbers had certainly dropped kindly for Albion and Liverpool. They had avoided a heavyweight collision at the hurdle often described as the most painful at which to fall. But the underdogs knew: If they were to lift the FA Cup for the first time in 14 years, they had to travel to face what Bill Shankly called the best club side in the world and deal with them in their own back yard.

And, despite the fighting words from inside Albion's dressing-room, their best chance of progress to the semi-finals had gone, as Bournemouth, Walsall and holders Tottenham could testify. All three had been drawn at home to the awesome Merseysiders in the 1967-68 Cup run, held their own and then been buried in replays amid the aura of Anfield.

The third trip of the season to 'Scouseland' meant Albion would have been watched by more than a quarter of a million spectators in their Cup run. And they were assured of another bumper following to the game when British Rail relaxed a hooligan-enforced ban on soccer specials by agreeing to lay on two 500-seater trains, complete with the dubious company of transport police and alsatians.

Places cost £1 and terrace tickets were on sale for four shillings (20p) for a game put back to nine days after the original meeting because of the England v Spain European Nations Cup clash in the normal replay week. The fact that Albion had no representatives in that Alf Ramsey squad and had the still uncapped Jeff Astle as their only serious contender underlined once more that it was every inch a team effort at The Hawthorns.

Tony Brown was still three seasons from his solitary England cap, Doug Fraser and Bobby Hope hadn't yet fulfilled either of the two appearances both made for the full Scotland side, Eddie Colquhoun wasn't capped by the Scots until he was a Sheffield United player in the early 1970s and John Kaye had not progressed beyond representing the Football League side.

In other words, Albion's only full internationals at the time were Welshmen

Graham Williams and Ronnie Rees, the latter of whom couldn't figure in the Cup run anyway. Liverpool had or had previously had Ian Callaghan, Roger Hunt and Peter Thompson in the England team and Tommy Lawrence, Ron Yeats and Ian St John in the Scottish line-up, with Chris Lawler, Emlyn Hughes and Tommy Smith all destined to follow them into the international ranks in the next couple of years. That's how strong they were.

Having secured the breakthrough with British Rail, Albion had to sort out their own engine room by getting Bobby Hope back on track. Bill Shankly's philosophy was simple: "Stop Hope and you stop Albion." His team hadn't had to deal with the brilliant schemer in the original game and weren't sorry to hear he was also struggling to play in the return.

The knee injury he had aggravated at Leicester on his comeback from a two-match absence meant he also had to sit out the next two League games - at home to Sunderland and away to Burnley. Albion's selection stability up to the turn of the year had become a thing of the past and changes continued to be forced on the Hawthorns management.

Captain Williams, who had a leg injury, also had to miss the Tuesday night visit of Sunderland but John Osborne proved his return to good health and, on a personal note, was content enough. He had kept a clean sheet on his comeback against Liverpool and added another against the Wearsiders but a scruffy 0-0 draw added up to a third successive poor League performance by the side.

Albion were undoubtedly being undermined by all the switches of personnel, the latest of them seeing Dennis Clarke drafted in again at right-back and Doug Fraser moved to left-back. Nick Krzywicki made way once more for Ronnie Rees while Eddie Colquhoun lined up at left-half as he had against Liverpool.

Try as they did against a Sunderland side three-quarters of the way down the table, Albion couldn't shake off the feeling that the bread-and-butter of League football was taking a back seat to the more exciting and instant demands of the FA Cup.

In a game played in a blizzard, they looked anything but the team who had scored more League goals (59 in 33 matches) than any First Division club other than Manchester United and Manchester City as they became bogged down in a bore of a 90 minutes. The defence again looked sure enough but Alan Ashman and Stuart Williams knew they would have to coax more urgency out of the attack to keep the FA Cup fires burning six days later.

And it was the same story from the same 11 at Turf Moor on the following Saturday, when Burnley made partial amends for the 8-1 Armistice Day mauling they had suffered at The Hawthorns the previous November. Dennis Clarke impressed at right-back and Osborne was a star in goal as he produced more of the form that was to prompt a transfer request from his deputy Rick Sheppard a few days later.

But, in the continued absence of Williams and Hope, there wasn't much else to enthuse over in Albion's performance apart from a sound return by John Talbut to the club where he had made a nightmare away debut for the Baggies with an own goal in a 5-1 defeat the season before.

Ron Potter was Albion's unused substitute on a day the side's form again started to cause concern. But they had their famous Cup fighting spirit, they had their lucky all white change strip and now they added the final ingredient of their 1967-68 success story - the bracing air of Southport, Ashman deciding against bringing his players back down the M6 from Burnley on the Saturday night.

Albion had headed for the coast in search of a pick-me-up the previous season with Jimmy Hagan as their manager and the relegation mire engulfing them. They certainly found one, subsequently collecting 18 points from 11 matches and almost reaching mid-table. Ashman's decision to follow suit for two nights of recuperation before the return with Liverpool showed he was not averse to carrying on the good ideas implemented by his predecessor.

Two men were not in the main party who checked in at the Prince of Wales Hotel a couple of streets behind the sea front. The recently sidelined Williams

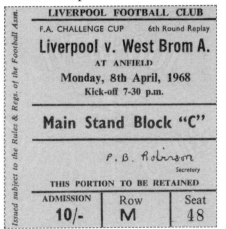

and Hope travelled separately by train and were photographed by the local Press as they left New Street on Sunday morning. Sheppard and winger Kenny Stephens also joined up late.

Albion had played seven games in the previous 28 days and had four League matches coming up in the space of only nine days. But the FA Cup was uppermost in their thoughts by now and there was no let-up. A massive hurdle awaited them the next night.

Monday, April 8

LIVERPOOL 1
Hateley 25
ALBION 1
Astle 68

LIVERPOOL   V   ALBION

Tommy Lawrence	1	John Osborne
Chris Lawler	2	Dennis Clarke
Emlyn Hughes	3	Graham Williams
Ian Ross	4	Doug Fraser
Ron Yeats	5	John Talbut
Geoff Strong	6	Eddie Colquhoun
Ian Callaghan	7	John Kaye
Roger Hunt	8	Tony Brown
Tony Hateley	9	Jeff Astle
Ian St John	10	Ian Collard
Peter Thompson	11	Clive Clark
(for St John, 114) Bobby Graham	12	Kenny Stephens (for Collard, 90)

Attendance: 54,273
Ref: J Carr (Sheffield)

Anfield Heroes

Bobby Hope's journey was in vain and he was on the sidelines for the sixth time in seven matches after failing a fitness test on his troublesome knee. Scottish manager Bobby Brown was disappointed as well, having hoped to have another look at him with a view to the games in Russia and Holland at the end of May. But Bill Shankly did not share the mood of letdown.

The Liverpool boss never regarded fear of complacency as a reason to spurn the chance of pumping even more confidence into his players and wasted no time telling his Liverpool team that Albion without Hope were like a magician without his bag of tricks. Not that the Hawthorns camp should have been surprised at the opposition manager's psychology.

When Shankly bumped into John Osborne in the Hawthorns tunnel before the League meeting of the clubs the previous September and learned that an injury had ruled the keeper out for the afternoon, he said as he turned towards the dressing-rooms: "Oh, it's going to be harder than we thought, then."

On a happier not for Albion, Graham Williams, the senior member of the Cup-chasing side and a man who had celebrated his 30th birthday on the day of the Sunderland game, was fit after a brief absence that Alan Ashman described as 'purely precautionary' in light of a leg injury. He took over the skipper and left-back duties from Doug Fraser, who returned to right-half on an evening on which Ronnie Rees again had to stand down.

Unusually, Rees's place on the right wing was occupied for considerable spells at Anfield by the workaholic John Kaye, with Tony Brown and Ian Collard on overtime in midfield. And, despite the tactical subtleties, Albion were magnificent against a team who only two days earlier had won in the League away to champions Manchester United.

If there was one day, or one night, on which West Bromwich Albion made a statement in that famous 1967-68 FA Cup run about being able to measure up against the very best, this was it. Stan Cullis, manager of the mighty Wolves in the 1950s and now boss of the Birmingham team awaiting the winners, was deeply impressed as he looked on with his assistant, Joe Mallett.

The outside world will see it as a night they somehow hung on for a third crack at Liverpool. But they headed home in the company of 10,000 of their fans, having again earned admiration from football's most renowned choral society, The Kop, and convinced themselves they might easily have managed another famous win at the red fortress. Bill Shankly wouldn't admit it but he was probably more relieved to escape with a draw than Alan Ashman was.

With Ron Yeats grounded and John Osborne off his line, Tony Hateley crashes a shot past no 6 Eddie Colquhoun to finally break the quarter-final deadlock with Albion and put Liverpool ahead at Anfield. Picture courtesy of the Liverpool Post & Echo.

For the fourth time in their run, gallant Albion had to save their Cup lives after falling behind and they were nursing something of a grievance as Tony Hateley broke a game-and-a-third goalless deadlock between the sides by crashing home a close-range shot in the 25th minute. They believed Ron Yeats was offside in the build-up as he headed against the bar from an Ian St John free-kick awarded for obstruction by Williams on Peter Thompson.

It was one thing to trail Colchester and Southampton (twice). It was another altogether to have to come back from behind against Liverpool on their own patch. Come back they did, though. They had been hit hard from the kick-off but the tide turned and the Baggies - again in all white although their blue and white stripes did not clash with the home side's all red - grew stronger.

Albion had to wait until the 68th minute for their equaliser but it was well deserved. The impressive Doug Fraser sent Tony Brown away down the right and his chip to the far post led to Jeff Astle extending his feat of scoring in every round so far as he beat full-back Chris Lawler to head past keeper Tommy Lawrence in front of a quietened Kop.

Liverpool had beaten Bournemouth 4-1, Walsall 5-2 and Tottenham 2-1 (after leading 2-0 into the last few minutes) in their earlier replays. Now, they knew they had a big battle and Albion could well have won the game towards the end of normal time as Brown slid in and narrowly failed to connect in front of goal with Fraser's right-wing centre.

Jeff Astle rises above full-back Chris Lawler to head a superb 68th minute equaliser from Tony Brown's right-wing cross and earn Albion a third crack at much-fancied Liverpool. The other home players in shot are Ian Ross (left) and Ian St John.

Liverpool continued to rock during the first period of extra-time - the first time the Baggies had been taken into an additional half-hour in FA Cup combat since their 2-1 defeat at Nottingham Forest in a 1962-63 fourth-round replay - and it was only after the sides had again switched ends that the famous and anticipated red surge materialised.

During that phase, John Talbut and Eddie Colquhoun, having kept Roger Hunt quiet and restricted Tony Hateley to only one clear chance, brilliantly put the squeeze on Shankly's danger-men and ensured there were no more goals. A grand total of 210 minutes of football had produced only one apiece.

Skipper Williams was a confident man as he puffed his chest out with pride afterwards and said: "Now we know we can win the FA Cup. I'm sure we can do it." Jeff Astle pulled no punches either. "We must reach the Final for Wembley's sake," he said. "Albion play attacking football but, if Liverpool meet Leeds or Everton in the Final, it will be the bore of the year. We now have a great chance of meeting Birmingham in the semi-final."

Albion still had plenty to do but this excellent performance - probably their best of the run to date despite their victory in adversity at Southampton - had raised their self-belief yet further. They might still have been underdogs to go through but some of the high ground Liverpool had seized by taking the tie to Anfield had been reclaimed. Everything remained to be played for.

It's Old Trafford!

It's one of the forgotten details of Albion's famous FA Cup journey that, in order to reach the semi-final, they nearly had to win at Old Trafford as well as emerge unscathed from Anfield. Not because they were ever drawn against Manchester United, even in an either/or pairing, but because the home of the then League champions was initially chosen to stage the third leg of the epic against Liverpool.

Talks between officials from the quarter-final opponents - that meant Alan Ashman, chairman Jim Gaunt and secretary Alan Everiss in Albion's case - established the prestige venue as a fair and appropriate destination for which to head next in a bid to end the compelling deadlock.

United, knocked out at the third-round stage by Tottenham, were also satisfied with the arrangement and pencilled the date of Thursday, April 18 into their schedule. It was only the next morning that they had second thoughts and came to the conclusion that they were cramming too much into Old Trafford's end-of-season programme.

They were again challenging hard for the title and had their sights set on becoming the first English club ever to win the European Cup. With three other big matches already fixed for their stadium around that time, they asked the FA if they could step down after all from Albion v Liverpool obligations.

The men at Lancaster Gate accepted their apology and restarted their considerations as to which neutral ground should stage the sixth round's only outstanding tie. Villa Park was too close to Albion and Goodison Park much too near to Liverpool and there was a reluctance to take tens of thousands of fans on unnecessarily long journeys to either London or Sheffield. For that reason, one venue stood out - the home of United's neighbours Manchester City.

With superstition so prevalent in the game, Albion were delighted with the choice. They had played brilliantly in winning 2-0 at Maine Road just after Christmas and had also bounced back from two down to take a vital point there the previous season. They had even won 5-1 away to a City in 1962-63. They would again have their lucky all white kit and they were heading for a lucky ground. So many good omens......

Albion were allocated 21,000 tickets for their eighth FA Cup game of the season - priced from 5s to 12s (25p to 60p) - and were to sell 17,000 of them. They already knew they would be heading for Villa Park if they reached the semi-final while Liverpool were on stand-by to travel to Hillsborough if it was they who faced Birmingham at the last-four stage.

Successive Cup trips to Merseyside and Manchester meant Albion were continuing to trawl the north of the country. Their earlier assignments in the competition had taken them to three different points south. Now, they had played at Burnley the previous Saturday and Anfield on the Monday and had to push on up the A1 in the same week with the Good Friday fixture list having handed them a long League trip to Newcastle.

Skipper Graham Williams had been nursed through at Anfield despite a knee injury and was rested at St James's Park, so Doug Fraser again moved into the joint job of stand-in left-back and stand-in captain. With Bobby Hope still out and aiming for the next instalment of the Liverpool saga, Tony Brown reverted to right-half and made way on the wing for Ronnie Rees.

It was just as well the Welshman faced Newcastle for he saved Albion from defeat. The side, back in all red in a clear indication that the white shirts and shorts were being saved only for the FA Cup, were two down by the 13th minute but, in a clear reversal of roles, the former Coventry winger headed in Jeff Astle's cross just after the hour. Then he fired low through a cluster of players after Ian Collard's 70th minute corner had reached him.

The 2-2 draw was satisfactory for a team competing with Newcastle for a place in the Inter Cities Fairs Cup via the League but who had other matters on their mind. It came at a high cost, though. Eddie Colquhoun badly damaged ligaments in his left ankle and, after being replaced by Ray Fairfax, was kept in hospital on Tyneside overnight. The Scot must have suspected it there and then: His FA Cup dream was over.

The former Bury defender had played 33 of the 35 League games and all of the League Cup and FA Cup ties apart from the two against Southampton in the latter. His outstanding contribution to the draw at Liverpool showed why he was so firmly established as a twin centre-half alongside John Talbut and made the £15,000 Jimmy Hagan had paid for him look good value indeed. Now, in one freak fall, he was out of the third match against Liverpool and out of the semi-final and final if Albion progressed that far.

"I went up for a header with Wyn Davies and felt something click in my ankle as I landed," he said. "I was in tremendous pain and thought I'd broken a bone." It was a sickening blow for the Scottish under-23 international. His Wembley aspirations were doomed and his Hawthorns star was to go into rapid decline from there.

Earlier this year, he confirmed: "I knew straightaway I wouldn't play again that season. My ankle was facing one way and my leg the other. I could tell that was me out for six months. When the Cup Final came round, it was probably easier for me to accept than if I had been touch and go, worked really hard to get fit and then just missed out. It was a big disappointment never to play at

Wembley but, as a Scot, I am bound to say that I did even better and played five times for my country at Hampden Park!"

Colquhoun's misfortune was confirmed in a Saturday phone call to Alan Ashman by the Newcastle United surgeon, who also happened to be the club's vice-chairman. The ligaments were so badly injured that the player's left leg was to be put in a plaster case for several weeks.

The news was a reminder that Albion were hitting problems wherever they turned. It was hard to believe they had fielded the same team for ten League games in a row in mid-season but that was before the start of the FA Cup run, which seemed destined to be plagued every inch of the way by adversity.

What Alan Ashman really needed was a good gap between fixtures. What he got was exactly the opposite. Albion, who also Jeff Astle, Clive Clark and veteran reserve full-back Ray Fairfax under treatment in the wake of the Newcastle game, travelled back from the north-east on the Friday evening and had a home game against Sheffield Wednesday the following afternoon!

And they had the return with Newcastle on the Monday, although that arrangement at least gave Colquhoun the opportunity to travel back to the West Midlands with Joe Harvey's sympathetic team. He did so sadly and on crutches.

Ashman was without Clark for the other Easter games, so Ronnie Rees moved to the left wing and Kenny Stephens played on the right. But Astle was fit to face Wednesday and headed his side's goal in the 1-1 draw. Williams's return had enabled Doug Fraser to revert to right-half and Tony Brown was pushed a little further forward. By far the most significant of all the positional changes, though, involved John Kaye.

He hadn't scored in the League since December 2 despite remaining a heroic worker and a brave, creative foil for Jeff Astle. But Colquhoun's lengthy absence opened new doors. Kaye was taken out of the front-line and used as a defensive left-half, almost alongside centre-half John Talbut. It was the role he had filled in emergency in the second half of the replay win at Southampton and his switch back there proved to be a master-stroke.

He stayed in the no 6 shirt for the rest of the season and was to emerge as a major star of the run-in, which continued with a 2-0 victory over Newcastle that was built on two first-half goals by Brown. The two points hoisted Albion back to seventh in the table and they had had a good Easter, albeit an exhausting and problematic one.

And their satisfaction was heightened by the return of Bobby Hope in the Monday game. He was brilliant in the first half against Newcastle despite a six-match absence and, as Bill Shankly knew, that wasn't good news for Liverpool.

Thursday, April 18

ALBION 2
Astle 7

Clark 60

LIVERPOOL 1
Hateley 39

ALBION   V   LIVERPOOL

ALBION		LIVERPOOL
John Osborne	1	Tommy Lawrence
Dennis Clarke	2	Chris Lawler
Graham Williams	3	Emlyn Hughes
Doug Fraser	4	Tommy Smith
John Talbut	5	Ron Yeats
John Kaye	6	Geoff Strong
Tony Brown	7	Ian Callaghan
Ian Collard	8	Roger Hunt
Jeff Astle	9	Tony Hateley
Bobby Hope	10	Ian St John
Clive Clark	11	Peter Thompson
(for Clarke, HT) Kenny Stephens	12	Peter Wall

Attendance: 56,139
Ref: J Finney (Hereford)

An Epic Victory

It was bordering on bare-faced cheek. FA Cup outsiders West Bromwich Albion weren't content to prepare back home in the West Midlands for their sixth-round second replay. They actually went deep into Liverpool territory - to the commuter town of Southport - to plot how they could finally bring down Bill Shankly's all-conquering team.

Alan Ashman had taken his squad there before the titanic game at Anfield and he saw no reason to deviate from that policy in the countdown to the third meeting. The desire for some clean seaside air and yet more team bonding saw to it that Albion's players were packing their bags once more on Easter Tuesday despite a gruelling sequence of six matches in 14 days.

Around 17,000 tickets for the Maine Road clash had been sold at the club by the time the team coach pulled away from The Hawthorns two days before match night. And it did so without an important piece of cargo - Clive Clark. The energetic left-winger had sat out the two home games over the holiday weekend with a pulled muscle that required further treatment.

As Liverpool battled to get their hard-man defender Tommy Smith fit for the first time since February 12 following a thigh problem, Albion were prepared to do all they could to have Clark ready. He broke down when he trained alone in West Bromwich the day before the game but even then no-one would rule him out. That's how important he was to the cause.

The former England under-23 international, who had tried his luck with hometown club Leeds and Huddersfield before being bought by Albion for £17,000 from QPR in 1961, travelled north on the Wednesday and was given a pain-killing injection aimed at getting his busy legs scampering across that spacious Manchester City pitch the following evening.

Clark's injury was yet one more to concern Alan Ashman and Stuart Williams but they took the gamble on him and decided Bobby Hope was fit as well after his comeback three days earlier. There was still a place for Ian Collard, though. He had been dropped to sub at home to Newcastle but was recalled to the starting line-up on the night Kenny Stephens was demoted to the bench and the cup-tied Ronnie Rees stood down.

With their first-choice attack back in place, Albion believed they could get at Liverpool. Bill Shankly's defence were rated as one of the most powerful in the game but there was a feeling in the Hawthorns camp that centre-half Ron Yeats was well past his best and a little vulnerable. Jeff Astle loved facing West Ham, Manchester United and Tottenham because of their defensive frailties and had more than a hunch he could cause the giant Yeats similar discomfort.

Ashman was restrained in his forecasts as he said of the third meeting: "It would be foolish of me to come out and say we will defeat Liverpool. You can never be that sure against a side of their all-round efficiency and strength. But we are prepared for another close, hard game and I can only repeat that we are pretty confident."

Tony Hateley, dropped for the League game at Sheffield United despite scoring against Albion in the first replay, was recalled and Maine Road fair crackled at kick-off, although Manchester's weather had done its worst for the big occasion. It was raining steadily and the more resourceful occupants of the open end of the ground turned their newspapers into emergency hats.

Albion may have been in Lancashire for more than 48 hours but they still struggled to get to the ground on time after their coach had been held up in huge traffic jams on the East Lancs Road. Surrounded en route by cars full of Liverpool fans, they were subjected to the predictable mickey-taking and found that a lot of Scousers appeared to think their side were going to win 2-0!

The team needed a police escort to get them through the busy streets to the packed stadium but, once the action got under-way, they were quickly out of the blocks. They drew first blood while many of the 56,139 crowd - the biggest of their Cup run to date - were still jostling for vantage points. Ian Collard provided the pass and Jeff Astle raced through with Chris Lawler in his wake

Tony Hateley is unmarked amid enormous Liverpool pressure as he plants his header past John Osborne to equalise at Maine Road. Picture courtesy of Liverpool Post & Echo.

to shoot low and left-footed under keeper Tommy Lawrence's near-post dive.

It was the first time Liverpool had been behind in the tie and Albion's fans held their breath in anticipation of the backlash. The big problem with scoring in only the seventh minute is that it gives the wounded favourite almost an hour and a half to bite back. And Liverpool soon showed their fangs. They didn't intend being behind for long.

Not for nothing were they fourth in the table and, with their matches in hand, still well in the hunt to regain the title they had won in 1963-64 and 1965-66. They produced waves of heavy pressure on Albion's beleaguered goal and, only three minutes after the breakthrough, came yet more injury disruption.

A sickening aerial clash with defensive partner John Talbut left John Kaye with a gash near his left eye-brow and in need of lengthy treatment. He played most of the rest of the match with his head bandaged and was to have ten stitches in the wound afterwards.

Such was the ferocity of the attacking into their faces that Kaye, perhaps momentarily disorientated because of his injury, smashed the ball against his own bar at one point while trying to turn back the red tide. Roger Hunt was also twice denied by fingertip saves by the diving John Osborne and, in a perverse way, it was almost a relief when the equaliser came in the 38th minute.

A left-wing corner was only partially cleared and the unmarked Tony Hateley headed down and across Osborne from Ian Callaghan's cross. The goal had been coming for so long that it felt like a sort of release; a cue from which the game could maybe regain some normality as far as Alan Ashman's battered warriors were concerned.

You would have got long odds at that point on Albion weathering the storm and going through. More so at half-time when they were forced into another change. A back injury meant right-back Dennis Clarke could not go out for the second half and, in the tactical reshuffle that followed, Kenny Stephens went on, Tony Brown moved from wide right into central midfield and Doug Fraser dropped from that area to right-back.

Albion were still acclimatising to the changes when Roger Hunt, who was having an excellent game, somehow failed to convert an inviting cross to the far post from Ian St John in the 46th minute. It was now a question of survival and consolidation for the Midlanders in a tie that throbbed with excitement and continued to contain some thrilling passages of play.

On this memorable Thursday night in Manchester, Bobby Hope showed just why he had always been rated so highly by Bill Shankly. His impact to date had by no means been all of an attacking nature but, bit by bit, he was seen more in his creative role and his influence on the game overshadowed that of Liverpool's own returning star, Tommy Smith.

Clive Clark squeezes the Maine Road winner past Tommy Smith and keeper Tommy Lawrence at the end of a brilliant Albion move.

Albion gained a fresh toehold, reasserted themselves and, with centre-half John Talbut sticking closer to Hateley than 'paper to the wall' in the eyes of one reporter, the tie swung back their way. They had trailed in round three to Colchester, in round four to Southampton (in two games) and in the round-six replay at Liverpool. Now, they were ready to strike out again in front.

They went ahead on the evening for the second and decisive time after 60 minutes when Fraser twice, Hope, Collard, Astle and Brown combined in a brilliant move that finally set Clive Clark free to score with a low left-foot shot as he was challenged by Lawrence and Smith. It was a terrific team goal, finished off in characteristic style by the winger who almost hadn't made it. Thank goodness Alan Ashman had waited another day for him!

It could soon have been 3-1 had a marginal offside decision not denied Stephens as he turned in Collard's cross following the midfielder's dash down the left. But the important thing was for Albion to keep the back door closed and that they did without the earlier alarms. Kaye, his head bandaged and his white shirt blood-spattered, reigned supreme and the dying minutes, although tense, were quite comfortable.

The final whistle blew on a famous victory and Albion had at last secured that mouth-watering semi-final against Birmingham. Their priceless spirit had hauled them through, in the face of great odds, a gruelling marathon against one of the country's most formidable sides. The players, absolutely exhausted, retreated to the dressing-room to congratulate each other and Kaye was famously photographed taking a puff of a welcome cigarette, sticking plasters covering a cut that required a hospital visit the next day.

He was described in one newspaper as a 'white-skinned Geronimo' and had obviously relished the battle. "We maybe didn't have chance to become nervous before the game because we were so late arriving," he recalled. "Then we took a bit of abuse from the Liverpool fans next to us in the traffic queues and that probably wound us up a bit more!

"I never got that excited about playing in London - perhaps because I am a northern lad - but I used to love playing against Liverpool and Everton because of the banter of the crowds. They always acknowledged you if you played well. It was a special night when we won at Maine Road. That and the first replay at Anfield were the sort of games you had to back yourselves in.

"It would have been easy for us to think we had missed our chance after the first game at The Hawthorns. We always felt under threat at set-pieces against Liverpool because they had Ron Yeats as well as Tony Hateley but, all along, we had a feeling we would get through and we all played well at Maine Road that evening. To make it to the FA Cup semi-final was a big breakthrough and we knew we had done it against the odds."

Kaye was enormous on that rainy night in Manchester, which proved to be the stage on which he reinvented himself in Albion colours. He had spent all his Hawthorns career to date as a centre-forward and inside-forward, forcing his way into Alf Ramsey's provisional World Cup 40 for the 1966 finals and, with his attacking partner Jeff Astle, seeing off the challenge of Ray Crawford.

The arrival of former Wolves and England man Crawford for £40,000 in 1965 meant Albion had the two costliest players in the Midlands in he and the £45,000 Kaye. It might seem small money by today's standards, but it was big then, even in American eyes, and the duo were dubbed the Million Dollar Babies when being introduced by one TV company during the 1966 visit to New York. The same station called the club West Bromwich of Albion!

Kaye, the son of a Goole docker, had been a prolific scorer earlier in his career, but still prone to barren spells. He netted 11 times in 27 League games in an injury-marred first season at the club and 18 in an ever-present 1965-66 campaign, only to fire a few blanks in 1964-65 (five goals in 25 League games) and 1966-67 (five in 40). Now, in emergency, he had been switched to the role of defender and was to remain there for the rest of his career.

With typical modesty, Kaye shrugged off his head injury - a forerunner to the one suffered by John Wile in the semi-final against Ipswich at Highbury ten years later - as 'one of those things.' It would have ended the involvement of a lesser man but he retreated briefly for repairs and couldn't wait to get back to the heat of the battle, quickly announcing his return with a meaty header!

As in the case of the stricken John Osborne at Southampton two months or so earlier, Stuart Williams was the man on hand to administer treatment and the trainer's theory about Albion having a better chance of beating Liverpool away from The Hawthorns had been justified.

"We played really well at Maine Road," he said. "Even Bill Shankly said we deserved to win, although he was choking on his words as he said it! I got on great with the likes of Ronnie Moran and Bob Paisley in their backroom team and it was wonderful to pit our wits against them and come out on top.

"John's injury was one more obstacle for the side to get over but they did that tremendously. He's a brave lad and played a full part in the victory. It's strange that I had had a couple of head injuries to deal with in my first few FA Cup matches with the first team and it was testimony to the lads that, each time, they overcame the setbacks."

It wasn't only Stuart Williams who had proved himself a decent forecaster. Jeff Astle backed up his optimism on the pitch with his seventh goal of the Cup run and again exposed Ron Yeats. The Liverpool centre-half was not used to defeat but says: "Although Jeff was a difficult opponent, I liked him because he was fair and a down-to-earth bloke - never a high-flier.

"The Cup games were real battles. We thought we should have beaten them and we hammered them at times at Manchester and just couldn't score. They had a good record at Anfield as well and we were left to reflect that, if you don't take your opportunities, you don't win. They stuck at it and went through. Give Albion half a chance in those days and they would score.

"We felt we peaked from 1963 to 1966 and then went into a bit of a decline, although we were still a very strong side. It was more painful for us losing that quarter-final because we would have had only Birmingham, a Second Division club, standing between us and an all-Mersey final against Everton. But Albion's win over us was their revenge for what had happened when we knocked them out of the Cup in 1965."

Liverpool had not taken defeat lightly. A police constable waited outside their dressing-room after the game and accused Tommy Smith of using abusive language in the dying minutes of the tie. Charges were likely to be brought until the player apologised and the matter was dropped.

Joe Mercer, manager of host club Manchester City, was one of the enthralled spectators and described Albion's performance as 'a great show.' "It should have been 3-1," he argued. "I will never know why Stephens' goal was ruled offside." And, because the match was being shown in a late-night highlights programme, the victorious players were able to watch their deeds on a portable TV on the coach afterwards, the biggest cheer greeting Clive Clark's winning goal.

Bobby Hope, whose first appearance in the drawn-out tie had proved to be a decisive one, has his own theory on why Albion emerged triumphant from the marathon despite having been held at The Hawthorns in the first game. "A lot of managers were fearful of going to Anfield and tended to change their tactics accordingly," he said. "We didn't. We had a good record up there.

"We had great pace in the side with Chippy Clark, who was never in the limelight like Jeff and Bomber but who was a terrific slip of a player. We had great attacking flair and their defence were often flat, so they were vulnerable to a ball over the top. I was in the stand at Anfield and thought the performance up there was outstanding.

"It was the same at Maine Road on a big pitch that suited us. But I still rate the win at Southampton as probably the best of the lot because we had Ossie injured from very early in the game and seemed to have everything against us. It was a great effort to pull through that night. Although Liverpool were a major force, we didn't have that sort of handicap when we played them."

After eliminating Liverpool, Albion felt no-one was going to stop them. If they could come emerge triumphant from that three-pronged test, they need fear no team - and that included two more northern powers in Leeds and Everton as well as their own local rivals and semi-final opponents Birmingham.

By slaying a giant, they had toppled another of the obstacles on the path to FA Cup glory. They had knocked out Liverpool, who in turn had knocked out Tottenham, who had knocked out Manchester United. Such is the way of things in knockout football. You either have to beat the best or beat a team who have beaten the best. Or both. Wembley was now one victory away.

A Bizarre Countdown

The path to the famous twin towers had opened up invitingly and, after surviving three gripping encounters with Liverpool, no-one begrudged Albion what appeared to be their easier task against Birmingham. It was a mammoth West Midlands occasion and there wasn't long to wait for it. The sixth round had been resolved only nine days before semi-final day.

Hosts Aston Villa, courtesy of many stirring battles highlighted by the replayed 1956-57 FA Cup semi-final against Albion, were seen as the Baggies' biggest rivals on the local patch, followed by Wolves. Blues were third in line when it came to parochial bragging rights but it was the huge stakes that made this game such a big deal. They were going head-to-head for a place in English football's main spectacle.

The crowd limit at Villa - then a Second Division club who were hurtling down towards the Third - was 61,000, some 5,000 down on normal because of ground repair work on the massive Holte End terrace. And, inevitably, tickets were snapped up in double-quick time as long queues formed at both clubs.

Albion soon won one battle with Blues when, on a visit to FA headquarters, Alan Ashman called heads, saw the coin drop kindly and so ensured his side would wear all white - also their opponents' preferred change colours. But they weren't as lucky in the allocation of dressing-rooms. They were given the away one.

Birmingham would have to wear a third-choice all red strip and hope that they fared better than Liverpool had in the same attire. Blues skipper Ron Wylie, a former colleague of Jeff Astle's at Notts County, quickly pointed out that his side had worn those colours in their victory against Halifax at the start of the Cup journey but he also saw danger looming.

"I went to Maine Road and was very impressed with Albion," he said. "What was significant about their victory was that they not only outplayed Liverpool, they also outran them." Wylie and his good friend Graham Williams were taken to Villa Park several days in advance and, dressed in full semi-final gear, were pictured shaking hands on the half-way line.

It was going to be a colossal collision and St Andrew's chairman Clifford Coombs said: "The match has set the city bubbling again. We wanted to meet Albion rather than Liverpool and are now assured of a Midlands club in the Final. Both clubs respect each other and it's almost a home game for us both."

On behalf of hosts Villa, Doug Ellis spoke of his pleasure in seeing Alan Ashman doing so well in his first season in the job while the manager's boss

Jim Gaunt, who had gone into the joyous Albion dressing-room at Maine Road and lit one of his trademark cigars, said: "I can't praise our boys highly enough. It has been a great effort to reach the semi-final."

Albion's had been the only one of the quarter-finals not to have been won and lost on its original date and Leeds - favourites for the Cup after beating Sheffield United 1-0 at Elland Road and booking a meeting with Everton at Old Trafford - were happy to see Ashman's men pushed to the limits of football endurance. They were to play them in the League on Saturday, April 20, only two days after the blockbuster at Maine Road.

And The Times reported that the home crowd showed their appreciation when Albion took to the field. It's doubtful whether the welcome was a tribute to the visitors' stirring FA Cup efforts. Much more plausible was the possibility that the Yorkshire folk were delighted and relieved at the elimination of a Liverpool side who had beaten Leeds in the 1965 Final!

There was yet more upheaval for the trip to Elland Road and not just because Ashman opted to miss the game so he could watch Birmingham's 0-0 Second Division draw at Crystal Palace. Not surprisingly, there was a price to pay in terms of injuries after the Liverpool marathon and no suspect player was going to be risked with the semi-final only a week away.

The changes were rung once more, with Bobby Hope (knee), Jeff Astle (knee), John Kaye (head), Clive Clark (leg) and Dennis Clarke (back) all out, Astle having started 45 of the previous 46 League and cup matches in the season and gone on from the substitutes' bench at Stoke when dropped for the other. A huge part of the team had again been ripped out.

Kenny Stephens was promoted from substitute and back came Ray Fairfax, Nicky Krzywicki, Ronnie Rees and Graham Lovett, the latter heading the goal of the game from Doug Fraser's cross, only for Leeds to comfortably win 3-1. Ray Wilson, who didn't kick a ball in the first team in either 1966-67 or 1967-68

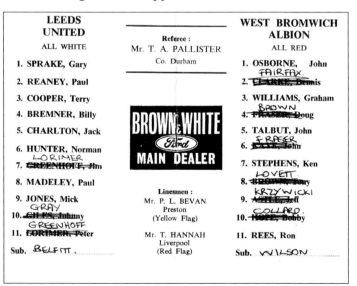

A much-changed line-up to visit and face the might of Leeds.

after making three senior appearances the previous season, was on the bench.

The line-up meant assistant boss Stuart Williams had a weakened hand as he found himself in charge for the day back at the ground where Albion's 1966-67 FA Cup hopes had been blown out of the water with a 5-0 fourth-round defeat that still stands as the club's heaviest in the competition.

Don Revie's men, who had already won the League Cup in 1967-68, were pushing hard for the title with the two Manchester foes and were also through to the final of the Inter Cities Fairs Cup. Their fixture schedule was even more demanding than Albion's but the telling difference at Elland Road was that the pursuit of League points mattered a lot more to one side than the other.

Albion's policy throughout the FA Cup campaign was to play League games normally and not 'save' themselves for sudden-death football. Nevertheless, given all their selection problems and the fact the decider against Liverpool had been only two days earlier, they lost little sleep over their defeat - their first in ten games in the First Division or FA Cup.

Thankfully, they now had a free week to prepare for the collision with Stan Cullis's Birmingham and the injured quintet were all expected to be fit with the possible exception of Dennis Clarke. At 20, the baby of the club's FA Cup squad had been struggling with his back since the League visit of Sheffield Wednesday and was making daily visits to a physio.

"I'm really anxious to be in the side providing I'm 100 per cent fit," he said. "I have been feeling better since I started hospital treatment and I'm hoping it will do the trick."

Blues had no injury problems other than midfielder Trevor Hockey, who was a long-term absentee with a broken ankle. Geoff Vowden and Colin Green missed their draw at Crystal Palace with a bruised thigh and a shoulder problem respectively but were declared fit at the start of a momentous week for the nation; the one which heralded the introduction of decimal currency and 5p and 10p pieces.

Jim Gaunt chose the build-up to the biggest Albion v Birmingham meeting since the 1931 FA Cup Final to announce that he would be standing down as chairman in 1969. And he accompanied his decision by expressing the wish that the position would go to Tommy Glidden, skipper of that victorious Baggies team of 37 years earlier and a man who joined the board on the same day as he did in 1951.

The 1968 Albion players weren't seeing much of their families amid the excitement of the Cup. Although the semi-final was to be fought out on the doorstep of they and their opponents, the now familiar trek to Southport was still on. One amendment Alan Ashman did make, though, was to delay departure until the Wednesday, having initially planned to go the day before.

There was an interesting gee-up at the club in midweek when youth coach Jimmy Dunn took the FA Cup winners' medal he had gained with Wolves in 1949 to the training ground. If the ploy to show off the spoils of success was a psychological move by Ashman and Stuart Williams to make their squad even hungrier, they must have been happy as a considerable cluster of players crowded round for a look at the cherished keepsake.

As news filtered through that 7s 6d (37p) semi-final tickets were changing hands for £5 thanks to busy touts, Dennis Clarke and Graham Williams sat out a pre-journey five-a-side practice match, the latter giving his team-mates a scare by reporting a slight reaction to the cartilage operation he had undergone on his left knee some months earlier. He complained of twinges and was given a pain-killing injection.

Bobby Hope caused a second fright when he landed heavily on his hip in a work-out. Thankfully, he was unhurt and Williams was to quickly allay fears as well by training well in front of a large crowd in the sunshine at Southport the following day, after which the players went off for a relaxing game of golf.

Ashman was able to report the encouraging news that all the injured players were fit. But, at the same time, skipper Graham Williams had bigger, much bigger, things on his mind - a remarkable kidnap threat against his wife Heather and their two young children.

The Albion and Wales left-back was friendly with several of Birmingham's players but appeared to have become the target of a Blues supporter prepared to attempt the meanest of ploys to gain his side every advantage possible. The threat to family members was something that was bound to occupy the thoughts of even a true professional like him.

"I wasn't a regular watcher of Albion games," Heather says. "I only went if they were semi-finals or finals, or if there was a party afterwards! Soon after the draw was made, I started getting phone calls from a chap saying I would be kidnapped along with the two children. At first, I thought it was a crank but, after telling the club, we informed the police and they took it seriously.

"Different officers came to stay with me and would go shopping with me. He or she would also take the telephone calls when they were in the house. We lived in Four Oaks near Sutton Coldfield at the time but I moved back to North Shropshire with the kids for a while."

It was a very worrying time for the family, even if daughter Kate and son Richard were too young at four and two respectively to comprehend what was going on. Dad still had to go to work and, in semi-final week, that just happened to be 100 miles away on the Lancashire coastline - an unfortunate situation that played on the skipper's mind.

"I couldn't accept that I was big enough to receive kidnap threats," Graham said. "That's something you associate with the very rich, like with the David Beckham business a few months ago. But I knew the police were there, so I was nothing like as worried as I would have been. Unfortunately, we didn't have a spare room, so the police officer left last thing every night and came back early next morning. There wasn't room for anyone from the force to stop over.

"Heather said she would move back to St Martin's and live with her mum. She was having more attention than I was anyway as the game came round. She was pictured going shopping to a supermarket in Moor Green with Ron Wylie's wife, Shirley, who we were friendly with, and picking the kids up from play school or wherever they were."

The police intercepted the would-be kidnapper's calls, which became more and more rare leading up to the tie. That eased Williams's apprehensions and it was decided it was safe for Heather to actually go to the match with her mother-in-law. "We had a sitter for the children and I remember I actually enjoyed the game," she said. "It was all very unpleasant in the build-up but, thankfully, it quietened down after the match had been played."

Villa Park was also to be used the following Thursday if a replay were needed and the police took no chances. They patrolled the stadium the evening before the game and made the surprise discovery of two cowering fans at 2am. The constabulary revealed that the hot breath of their alsatians ensured that the intruders left the ground even quicker than they had entered!

One of the benefits of Albion's players being at Southport was that it kept them away from where the talk about the game was at its most intense. Alan Ashman was happy that his squad were detached from the huge FA Cup fever engulfing local communities and were able to keep their heads relatively clear, even though the local shop-staff who taunted them on the way to training before the game against their beloved Liverpool with shouts of 'Up the Reds!' were now wishing them well.

The threats to the Williams household were something Albion could well have done without but the skipper was still able to see the merits of preparing for the semi-final so far from home. "Blues stayed local, so they were more in the public eye and easier for the media to reach and interview," he added. "We did not feel that same pressure from supporters."

Fourteen Albion players were part of that particular exodus, including Ronnie Rees, the club record signing who couldn't play for them in the Cup that season. And, when they returned down the M6 following a Friday seven-a-side session, they still didn't see their homes. They were whisked to a Stafford hotel to keep them away from potential distractions.

With ten of the places filled, it was a toss-up whether right-back Dennis Clarke or right-winger Kenny Stephens would be handed the other. Doug Fraser and Tony Brown had a vested interest as their roles hinged on the selection. If Stephens got the nod, it would be business as usual. If Clarke played, they would both be used in more advanced positions at right-half and on the right wing respectively.

The clash with Birmingham brought Fraser back into combat with the club against whom he had made his debut in a 3-1 win at The Hawthorns in 1963, after arriving in the game as a late starter. He was born in a Lanarkshire village called Busby, near Glasgow, but didn't play any organised football until he was 16.

"I was always very keen to play but never had the chance at school," he recalled. "I did a milk round at

Doug Fraser - running out to face Blues again five years after his Albion debut against them.

five in the morning and, after I'd come home in the afternoons, I did a busy grocery round, pushing a wheelbarrow round the streets! I would still play a bit of kickabout football because I was a fit lad but it was only after I'd started work as an apprentice engineer in the tool-room of Rolls Royce in East Kilbride that I started to play properly.

"They had a team there and I did well enough to join a club called Eaglesham Amateurs, where I played as a centre-forward. I was still playing up front when I joined Aberdeen but I think I only appeared in one match for them in that position before I started to be seen as a wing-half."

Fraser stacked up more than 70 first-team appearances for Aberdeen in the top flight before Albion's highly successful trawling of the country brought him to their attention. Paddy Ryan is the man credited with his 'spotting' and it wasn't long before Jimmy Hagan was touching down in the granite city with a cheque-book and a determination not to travel home alone.

"It was a great surprise when the chance came to join Albion," the player added. "A few years earlier, it was the last thing on my mind. But I made the move and came down to The Hawthorns a few years behind other Scots lads like Bobby Hope, Kenny Foggo, Campbell Crawford and Bobby Murray.

"It turned out to be a terrific move for me but it wasn't all plain sailing. I have to confess to worrying for a while whether I had done the right thing because the players were so much fitter and the English game so much faster. I wondered whether I would be able to cope but, thankfully, my own fitness and game sharpened up."

Come semi-final time, Fraser was one of the solid fixtures in Albion's team, having missed only one League game that season (at Coventry in September) and played well over 30 in each of the previous three, including the maximum 42 in 1965-66. He was very much the solid dependable type Alan Ashman felt he could turn to amid the tension of an interesting last-four line-up.

If Everton were the youngest of the four semi-finalists and Leeds the most experienced and battle-hardened, Albion's opponents Birmingham City were certainly the dark horses. Under the management of legendary former Wolves manager and skipper Stan Cullis, they were, all said and done, a Division Two side and could hardly be bracketed alongside the Baggies' previous victims Liverpool.

They had shown their liking for knock-out football, though, by reaching the semi-final of the 1966-67 League Cup before losing over two legs to eventual winners QPR. "I'm not going to say, just because we have beaten Arsenal and Chelsea, that our ideas will work again when we play Albion," Cullis said. "All we can do is plan our tactics as carefully as possible and hope they are the right ones."

Against Albion, they opted to use full-back Colin Green, who had marked Stanley Matthews on his League debut when playing for Everton a few years earlier, as a stand-in inside-forward. Green was to win 15 caps for Wales, keeper Jim Herriot played eight times for Scotland and ex-Chelsea winger Barry Bridges - a former England schoolboys team-mate of John Osborne and John Talbut - was the holder of four senior caps.

Experienced left-half Malcolm Beard was an England youth international of the past, centre-forward Fred Pickering represented England three times in the mid-1960s and Ron Wylie was back on familiar territory for the semi-final, having been named 1964-65 Midland Footballer of the Year when an Aston Villa player.

Blues, for whom another one-time Chelsea man, Bert Murray, had been converted from a right-winger to right-back, had talent in their ranks and they even had a West Bromwich lad, inside-forward and England youth international Johnny Vincent, to call upon from the substitutes' bench. But the bottom line was that they were a Second Division club and one who, despite the scoring of 78 League goals to that point, had suffered a slump and had already virtually kissed goodbye to their hopes of promotion.

Pickering, denied FA Cup glory with Everton in the 1966 Final by injury before joining Blues in the summer of 1967, had been doubtful with a thigh problem - not a 'thing' problem, as one of the newspapers amusingly called it! He recovered in good time, though, and was seen as the main danger to confident Albion.

He had scored twice in his side's Cup run, including the only goal of the quarter-final triumph against Chelsea. And, although Geoff Vowden, who lost his wife to a terminal illness at the start of April, and Barry Bridges had netted four times each on the road to Wembley, he carried many of the hopes at a club who had been watched by 51,586 in their fifth-round replay win at home to Arsenal and 52,500 against Chelsea in the next round.

John Kaye insists he never doubted that Albion would win, although he recognised that the derby occasion added another degree of trickiness to their task. Skipper Graham Williams was every bit as assured. "We didn't fancy Jim Herriot," he said. "He used to black under his eyes to stop the glare when he was playing under floodlights but he wasn't that big, so we knew he couldn't compete with Jeff Astle.

"We thought John Talbut and John Kaye could outjump and outfight Fred Pickering, while Barry Bridges and Bert Murray weren't the players they had been. We considered each player on either side individually and we knew Blues couldn't measure up if we played somewhere near our best."

There was a note of apprehension, though, in what Williams went on to say: "None of our side have ever reached the last four of the FA Cup. I know we have done well in the League Cup but there's a lot more tension surrounding this competition. This is a Midlands cup final as well as the FA Cup semi-final. It's the most important match I have ever played in and that includes all my internationals. Nerves will play a big part and Blues have several players who have been on this stage before like Fred Pickering, Ron Wylie, Barry Bridges and Bert Murray."

Publicly at least, Alan Ashman was less precise in his summing-up of how the biggest West Midlands derby clash for many years might go. "We know it's going to be extremely hard," he said. "Any local derby is difficult and the fact this is an FA Cup semi-final makes it doubly hard.

"We have the greatest respect for Birmingham and there will be no question of over-confidence in our thinking. There can't be. We learned that much at Colchester and it was a valuable lesson for us all. We escaped with a draw and we were lucky to do so. We might never have come as far as we have in the competition."

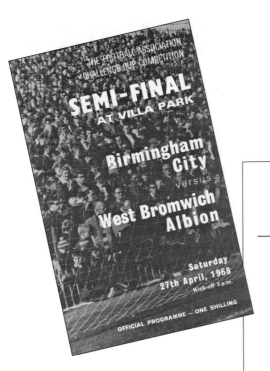

Saturday, April 27

BIRMINGHAM 0

ALBION 2
Astle 13
Brown 67

BIRMINGHAM   V   ALBION

Birmingham		Albion
Jim Herriot	1	John Osborne
Bert Murray	2	Doug Fraser
Ray Martin	3	Graham Williams
Ron Wylie	4	Tony Brown
Winston Foster	5	John Talbut
Malcolm Beard	6	John Kaye
Geoff Vowden	7	Kenny Stephens
Colin Green	8	Ian Collard
Fred Pickering	9	Jeff Astle
Malcolm Page	10	Bobby Hope
Barry Bridges	11	Clive Clark
(for Green, 65) Johnny Vincent	12	Dennis Clarke

Attendance: 60,831
Ref: K Howley (Billingham)

Derby-day Delight

Philip Bleiberg, at 58 then the world's most successful heart transplant patient, revealed in The Times of late April, 1968, what he longed to do now he was feeling better: Go back to swimming nude at the men-only bathing area of Graaf's Poll in Cape Town! Elsewhere in the posh people's paper, Geoffrey Green was showing a different kind of brazenness.

The contents of his preview of that day's FA Cup semi-final action could be said to be more conservative but it was the headline that did most to grab the attention: West Brom to beat Everton in the Final. As ever, one of Fleet Street's finest had written it beautifully - but had he also called it correctly?

As last-four day dawned, Leeds were Cup favourites, having engineered the chance of becoming the first club ever to reach the finals of the two domestic knockouts in the same season. They had followed Albion and QPR as holders of the League Cup and were now well fancied to overcome Everton at Old Trafford in the bigger competition.

Many thought the Toffees were about to come unstuck, not least because they were without their main midfield inspiration Alan Ball through suspension and youngster John Hurst through jaundice while Leeds had Johnny Giles back in their engine-room after injury.

At Villa Park, Dennis Clarke didn't make Albion's starting line-up, Alan Ashman leaving him on the bench and handing Kenny Stephens the right-wing role. It was the young Bristolian's first FA Cup start, although he had scored in a League Cup tie at home to Manchester City when making his senior debut 18 months earlier.

This was an altogether grander stage, the biggest game of his career, and he said: "I was really thrilled to be in the team. But, despite all the tension of the semi-final and derby day, I didn't feel any more keyed-up than I did before any other game."

The wives of Albion's players were impressed at being handed travel rugs for extra comfort as they took their seats at an overcast Villa Park. But they were soon up on their feet. As at Maine Road,

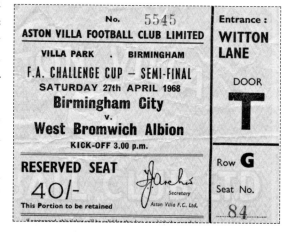

No. 5545

ASTON VILLA FOOTBALL CLUB LIMITED

VILLA PARK . BIRMINGHAM

F.A. CHALLENGE CUP — SEMI-FINAL
SATURDAY 27th APRIL 1968

Birmingham City
v.
West Bromwich Albion

KICK-OFF 3.00 p.m.

RESERVED SEAT

40/-

This Portion to be retained

Secretary
Aston Villa F.C. Ltd.

Entrance :

WITTON LANE

DOOR

T

Row **G**

Seat No.

84

Bobby Hope leaps in delight, Graham Williams spreads his arms and Clive Clark heads towards Jeff Astle after the no 9 had broken through Birmingham's defence early on.

the side had a perfect start, Jim Herriot going down to his right to beat away Tony Brown's shot following a short pass by Bobby Hope, only for Jeff Astle to run in from the left and slot home.

Only 13 minutes gone and the centre-forward's goal-in-every-round record had been extended, albeit from a dubious free-kick awarded for a challenge on him by Winston Foster on the edge of the area. There was also a touch of irony. Stan Cullis, as Wolves manager, had travelled to watch Astle play for Notts County at Newport in 1964 but Jimmy Hagan nipped in to sign him after no fewer than six scouting trips.

Albion had already gone close with Clive Clark rising well to nod just over from Ian Collard's centre but it said much for Birmingham's fightback that John Osborne became as impressive a performer as there was on the field. He made a flying backwards leap to keep out Fred Pickering's early header, then soared to his left to palm a shot from the same player on to the woodwork, the ball rebounding into his grateful arms.

The keeper, who had been cup-tied for Albion's League Cup Final defeat the previous season, was doing plenty to earn a trip back to Wembley in the FA Cup. He also had to plunge at the feet of Geoff Vowden, clutch a header by Pickering that flew straight at him and say a quiet word of thanks to John Talbut, who used all his experience and anticipation in clearing off the line from the unlucky Pickering in the second half.

Albion conceded twice as many free-kicks and three times as many corners

Jeff Astle and Clive Clark follow up just in case but all they have to do is show their joy as Tony Brown's shot beats Jim Herriot's dive for Albion's second semi-final goal.

as their opponents and managed only four clear scoring attempts to the nine by Blues. But maybe the Second Division club picked an over-defensive side that meant some of the half-chances fell to players who were not natural finishers.

Bridges squandered a decent opening and Johnny Vincent's confinement to the bench at the start was perhaps a surprise given that he was on the way to a goal haul for the season of 14. Even so, the impressive Ron Wylie was proud of his side and said: "If just one chance had gone in when it was still 1-0, it could have set the game alight. Anything might have happened."

But the game was confirmed as won and lost in the 67th minute following a poor pass by Bert Murray that enabled Brown to exchange passes with Hope before producing a tremendous right-foot angled drive. The ball struck the foot of the far post and, as if to confirm that it was Albion's day, cannoned into the Witton End net rather than out to safety.

John Kaye, having struggled for goals when played in attack for most of the season, moved forward from his new defensive station and crashed a shot past the diving Jim Herriot with his unfavoured left foot in the second half. He would love to have been on the score-sheet but it hardly mattered in the bigger picture that the effort was disallowed for an infringement.

Albion, with Talbut and Osborne the stars, were more than content with their two-goal victory. In many ways, the game had been an anti-climax after the heights of the quarter-final but they weren't overly concerned. Semi-finals are rarely classics. Winning is all that matters and victory was theirs to toast. Talbut

Vital intervention from the outstanding John Talbut as he clears off the line in the second half from Fred Pickering, watched by a grateful John Osborne and John Kaye.

did that by lighting up a cigarette in the dressing-room; another sure sign that football was far different then!

Ashman admitted: "I didn't think it was a great game. This one had the added tension of being a local derby and we are hoping to produce much better form at Wembley." Birmingham assistant Joe Mallett reflected sadly: "We did everything we set out to do apart from putting the ball in the net when we had the chances."

The result reinforced Albion's self-belief and skipper Graham Williams, who made no special getaway in view of the kidnap threat against his family, said: "We knew Blues' strength was getting balls into Pickering, so we said we would be all right if we could cut off the supply line. Ossie told us they wouldn't score and he came and took everything. He was a giant that day.

"I couldn't remember a good semi-final and I couldn't argue that this one was because there was so much at stake. It's how you handle the tension that counts. We were more nervous of that game because we were expected to win and it seemed we always let ourselves down when we were favourites, as we had against QPR. It was a mission achieved just to be at Wembley."

Victory meant Albion would equal Newcastle's record of ten FA Cup Final appearances. The wait for a return trip to football's showpiece game had spanned 14 long years, during which the only town representation had been when West Bromwich's Bill Clements refereed Liverpool's 1965 victory over Leeds.

Leeds would not be going back in 1968. Confirmation that this was the year of the underdog came when Everton profited from a mistake by Gary Sprake - a Welsh international colleague of Graham Williams - and won the other semi 1-0 at Old Trafford. The keeper's poor clearance was chipped towards goal by Jimmy Husband, Jack Charlton handled near the line and Johnny Morrissey struck home the penalty.

"We were glad when we heard in the dressing-room afterwards that Everton had won," skipper Williams added. "Footballers are a superstitious breed and it's often said that no team can beat another three times in one season. We went along with that theory and weren't worried about facing them at Wembley.

"Everybody was happy. Playing in the FA Cup Final is every player's dream and I had heard lots at the club about the 1954 Final. That side almost won the double and we youngsters had such respect that we called them Mr Allen, Mr Barlow and Mr Dugdale. I used to caddy for Ronnie when he played golf at Sandwell Park or Handsworth on a day-off and I hated it. So did Alec Jackson and we both took up squash instead!"

Williams didn't have Albion's 1968 apprentices running round for him in the same way but his pride as a captain bound for Wembley was obvious.

The stars of 1954 had become team-mates of his. Now, he had the chance to emulate their 3-2 FA Cup Final victory over Preston. It was an opportunity and experience he didn't intend to pass up.

Ian Collard in a semi-final tangle with Ron Wylie at Villa Park.

Wembley Warm-up

Albion's semi-final victory had generated record Villa Park gate receipts of £37,028 and, inevitably, the Final immediately proved big business. As early as the following Monday morning, it was announced that the Wembley showdown against Everton was to be televised live on both BBC1 and BBC2 and, for the privileged few, in a luxury new form: In colour!

The big game was still over two and a half weeks away but there were early signs that everyone would want a piece of Albion. A Cup Final dance was arranged at West Bromwich's Adelphi Ballroom for Thursday, May 9, and talk of a post-match civic reception to be hosted by the Mayor of West Bromwich, Alderman C O Ellis, had already kicked off.

On a smaller scale, the first-team squad were each presented with a portable typewriter by a company in the town, then an intricate blue and white cake depicting the Cup Final scene was presented to Alan Ashman's squad by the renowned and long-established confectionery firm, Firkins. As a charitable gesture befitting weight-conscious athletes, the players found a better home for the offering than their own stomachs - West Bromwich District Hospital.

Albion also had all the familiar media duties to plan for in the three weeks before their revenge mission against Everton and anticipation was building. The club were on their way to a final League placing of eighth - their best for nine years other than their sixth spot in 1965-66 - but midfielder Bobby Hope considered the cups to be the side's forte.

"Cup football is so different to the League," he said. "Our style of play is best suited to the sudden-death competitions and I also believe we are more mature, man for man, than Everton. We, like Manchester United, Manchester City and West Ham, have attacking players through the team, which means we have to play attacking football. It should be one of the most entertaining finals since the war, although this will be little consolation to us if we lose."

On a personal note, Hope could afford to feel happy with his contribution and added: "This has been my best season since I joined the club nine years ago. A Cup winners' medal is the ambition of every professional but I will never feel I have really reached the pinnacle of the game until I have won a full Scottish cap."

The only down-side to his campaign was that he had netted just five times. In 1964-65, the Scot bet manager Jimmy Hagan that he would score more goals than Sir Stanley Matthews - a feat he duly managed, although he didn't get off the mark until the game with Villa at The Hawthorns in late February.

Taking delivery of a Wembley cake from renowned confectioners Firkins are (from left) Graham Lovett, chairman Jim Gaunt, Graham Williams, Bobby Hope and Clive Clark.

Hagan was surprised Hope didn't score more often because, for a player full of neat turns, deft chips and immaculate distribution, he also had a terrific shot. Fortunately, with Jeff Astle, Tony Brown and Clive Clark, Albion had others to shoulder the scoring burden while Hope remained a creator of high quality.

The club still had four more League fixtures to squeeze in and, typical of that manic spring, the first of those came just two nights after the celebrations of semi-final day. It wasn't any old First Division assignment either, Albion having to face a Monday night visit from a Manchester United side who were still in the European Cup and still in contention to retain their League title.

The public had been slow to warm to the success of Alan Ashman's side that season, with four of their home matches failing to pull in 20,000 and four more struggling just past that mark. On that utterly exhilarating evening, though, The Hawthorns vibrated to the sound of 45,992 - a packed house who were treated to a quite pulsating game.

Ashman rested John Kaye because of a touch of flu and gave Clive Clark more time to shake off the after-effects of a troublesome thigh muscle injury. Kenny Stephens also stood down and Ronnie Rees returned, along with Asa Hartford (for his first home start) and Dennis Clarke, while Doug Fraser switched to left-half.

Albion had played brilliantly without reward in their 2-1 defeat at Old Trafford in December. In the return, they were even better and extracted maximum pay-back. They thrashed the champions 6-3 and, with a few minutes remaining, were five goals ahead of the team who had beaten Real Madrid 1-0 in the first leg of the European Cup semi-final the previous week. It was sensational, breathless stuff.

Where Albion found their energy from in the wake of their semi-final exertions is anybody's guess. It could easily have become a case of after the Lord Mayor's Show but, instead, they were ahead in nine minutes and four up before Denis Law pulled one back from a penalty. Brian Kidd scored twice late on for a side also containing George Best, Bobby Charlton, Nobby Stiles and Pat Crerand but their heaviest mauling for five years was already guaranteed.

Jeff Astle, who could do no wrong in the FA Cup, wasn't bad in the League either. He scored his seventh hat-trick for the club and so went top of the First Division marksmen list by taking his tally for 1967-68 past 30. It meant he had established a mark that was to remain his highest goal total in a season in his ten years at The Hawthorns.

Unbelievably, he had to wait only two more nights for another treble. The fare wasn't quite as heady but, by any other yardstick, super-charged Albion were still terrific as they caught up with their unkind fixture backlog with another victory, this time 3-1 at home to West Ham.

Despite the elation of the previous four days, the gate for the clash with the Hammers was 20,000 down on that for the Manchester United match - further evidence of the struggle Albion had to pull in the masses for bread-and-butter fixtures. But the football compensated on an evening when young Alan Merrick would have made his debut had it not been for an ankle injury.

There was the usual chopping and changing to the team, with Doug Fraser and Tony Brown forced to rest thigh injuries and Graham Williams again pulled out of the firing line because of his on-going knee problem. John Kaye was in good health, though, Graham Lovett's promotion from the sub's bench restored him to his old right-half position for the first time in 1967-68 and Ray Fairfax was recalled at full-back.

That match-day of May 1 wasn't only important to the players. It was also the deadline for postal applications for Cup Final tickets and, with demand already having gone through the roof, secretary Alan Everiss announced: "No further applications can be accepted from any source."

Off the field, Albion received the news they wanted when the FA informed them they would be playing in their all white change strip at Wembley. Anything else would have been unthinkable! Everton would also change - from the first-choice blue and white they had worn in their 1966 Cup Final victory

113

over Sheffield Wednesday to the amber shirts and blue shorts they had used in winning 6-2 at The Hawthorns..

In their final home match of the season, Albion even survived the shock of falling behind to a third minute goal from Martin Peters. Astle outjumped John Cushley to head the equaliser from Bobby Hope's corner mid-way through the first half and, despite being dazed, produced another terrific leap to float a header over keeper Bobby Ferguson from Asa Hartford's right-wing centre eight minutes later.

Alan Ashman's side were oozing class and confidence and Astle started the move that brought the clinching goal early in the second half. He laid off a pass to the right to Hope then moved into the middle to meet the schemer's cross and steer it home. For the second time, the fans' favourite had scored two hat-tricks in a week, the other in September, 1965, when his League trebles against Sheffield Wednesday and Northampton came either side of a 3-2 win at Everton in which he had an off night and scored only once!

Astle was left with swelling beneath his right eye following his buffeting against the Hammers and said: "My whole face went numb and it felt as though I had had all my teeth out. But, otherwise, I feel great! I'm on top of the world because I'm playing better now than at any stage in my career."

Albion's performance, not least Astle's red-hot streak, provided food for thought for former Hawthorns coach Wilf Dixon, who was at the game, along with his boss Harry Catterick, in his new role as part of the Everton backroom team. On a night when John Osborne and John Talbut again impressed, Ian Collard's fine form in midfield went a long way to securing his Wembley place despite the struggle he had to win over some fans.

It was an invigorating time at the club and the mood of happiness and excitement was compounded when Eddie Colquhoun's wife presented him with a baby at Dudley Road Hospital. To a man, the dressing-room sympathised with the Scot over the injury that had ended his season and were delighted that life at home was kinder, albeit now more hectic.

Albion had shown they could win - and win brilliantly - in the absence of several first-teamers and had all their injured players, apart from Colquhoun, fit for the trip to Sunderland the following Saturday. How Bobby Robson must have envied Ashman! The former Baggies wing-half's Fulham team had just been condemned to relegation by a home defeat against Stoke.

As they were preparing to set off for the north-east, Albion heard that Leo Callaghan had been chosen as Cup Final referee. The 43-year-old child care officer from Merthyr Tydfil was the first Welshman to be handed the honour since Mr M Griffiths of Newport had taken charge of the 'Matthews Final' between Blackpool and Bolton in 1953.

Callaghan did not lack big-match experience. He had officiated the Portugal v Hungary game at Old Trafford in the 1966 World Cup, a Scotland v England clash at Hampden Park and, earlier in 1967-68, the England v Northern Ireland match at Wembley. He had taken ten full internationals in all, six Welsh Cup finals and some European ties, and would have William Johnson (Kendal) and John Homewood (Sunbury-on-Thames) as linesmen.

Jeff Astle had more recognition of his own. He was named Player of the Month by a London evening newspaper after his astonishing scoring burst of seven goals in three matches but his golden spell ground to a halt at Roker Park as Albion and Sunderland fought out their second goalless draw in just over a month.

The striker was subdued and almost anonymous as Alan Ashman decided after all to keep Tony Brown in reserve and take no chances with Bobby Hope, who had suffered a kick on the thigh against West Ham. The honours in front of a 31,892 attendance at Roker Park went to defenders, with John Osborne again immaculate and John Kaye, John Talbut and Doug Fraser running him close for top billing.

With 1965-66 League Cup finalist Ray Fairfax playing the last of his 92 first-team games before joining Northampton, Graham Williams was also able to put his feet up on a day Sunderland twice struck the woodwork. But a feature of the game was the full throttle Albion gave it. Although Wembley was only a fortnight away, they couldn't be accused of slacking.

They had also demonstrated the new hard-to-beat quality they had acquired under Alan Ashman and Stuart Williams. Their fifth goalless draw in just over two months meant they had lost only two of 22 games in League and Cup and conceded just 26 goals in the process, six of them on one freak afternoon at home to Everton.

A newspaper image of John Osborne's assured handling in the 0-0 draw at Sunderland.

A couple of days after the long trip to Roker Park, it was revealed that Princess Alexandra - a first cousin to the Queen - would be guest of honour on FA Cup Final afternoon.

She would meet the players before kick-off and then present the Cup and medals afterwards. Graham Williams had his sights set on keeping a very special royal appointment at around 4.50pm on Saturday, May 18, but still had a little bit to do to ensure he would be walking up those steps, either as a winner or a loser.

He followed up his absence from the matches against West Ham and Sunderland by also withdrawing from the Welsh team to face West Germany at Cardiff in midweek. It wasn't a decision he took lightly despite the need to be fit for his club. He knew the curtain was beginning to fall on his international career and said: "I'm very disappointed to have to turn down the invitation."

Ronnie Rees was able to link up with his country as, back in the West Midlands, Alan Ashman staged a Tuesday five-a-side match that included all of his recent casualties. What's more, they emerged unscathed to keep a smile on the friendly face of their manager.

The FA, meanwhile, were attending to the usual formalities and decided on Hillsborough as the venue for an FA Cup Final replay on Thursday, May 23, should one be needed. That was rubbing it in for Sheffield Wednesday fans. Their team had lost to Everton in the 1966 Final; now there was a chance they would have a close-up of the same club celebrating 1968 victory as well.

The replay contingency also had a thorny edge for Albion. They were due to depart on their end-of-season tour to East Africa on the Tuesday after Wembley and had already had to cancel the first of the tour matches - a clash with Nairobi in the Kenyan capital scheduled for Cup Final day.

Albion had another reminder of the size of their task at the twin towers when Everton trio Ray Wilson, Brian Labone and Alan Ball played in a 2-1 win against Spain in Madrid's Bernabeau Stadium that put England through to the quarter-finals of the European Nations Cup. There were no representatives from The Hawthorns in Alf Ramsey's side, nor, indeed, any from the Midlands.

The lucky fans who had secured Final tickets were busy making their travel arrangements and, for Albion supporters, there was the option of jumping aboard one of the special trains laid on by British Rail. Prices ranged from 82s 6d (£4.25) for those who wanted a meal each way in the dining car to 32s 6d (£1.60) just for a seat. Either way, there was determination to make a full day of it. The first departure to Wembley Central was to be at 7.10am!

By coincidence, both Albion and Everton had a dress rehearsal for their big meeting when they each had appointments in London as the Football League season ended on the Saturday before the Final. Highbury and Upton Park were their respective destinations and the team choices of the two managers provided an interesting talking point.

Everton's Harry Catterick took no chances and decided to rest Gordon West, Joe Royle and the England trio of Brian Labone, Alan Ball and Ray Wilson for the trip to West Ham. The fact that his side still drew 1-1 with their mid-table opponents underlined what a substantial obstacle they represented in the FA Cup Final. But the respect was mutual.

"We are all ignoring the 6-2 victory we had at The Hawthorns in the League," said the Merseysiders' star man Alan Ball. "We know Albion can be a great side and we're expecting to see evidence of that from them when we meet at Wembley."

The Baggies' 'main man' Jeff Astle had more good news on the last day of the First Division season when he edged out Birmingham skipper Ron Wylie in being named Evening Mail Midlands Footballer of the Year - an honour he attributed to the shock of being dropped for the autumn game at Stoke and then being part of a side castigated by their manager following a dire 4-2 defeat at Coventry.

A few miles north west of where Everton were going into action with shadow players such as goalkeeper Geoff Barnett and right-winger Gerry Humphreys, Alan Ashman opted to field his big guns for the visit to an Arsenal side who had won their previous four games and scored 11 goals in the process.

Having rung the changes for many weeks - in most cases when he had no choice - he opted for a line-up that was interpreted by many as a strong clue to the make-up of his Wembley team. Indeed, the manager said his Highbury side would be 'very close' to that for the return excursion to London the following Saturday, although Dennis Clarke, having lined up at no 2 in the previous three matches, was perturbed at being left behind to play instead for the reserves at home to Newcastle.

John Osborne was also omitted - replaced by Rick Sheppard after suffering a reaction to a midweek smallpox vaccination - but Graham Williams, Tony Brown and Bobby Hope were all back. Graham Lovett's inclusion on the right wing at the expense of Asa Hartford, Nick Krzywicki, Kenny Stephens and Ronnie Rees, was a particularly strong signal. The gates to the famous stadium appeared to be swinging open for the young Brummie.

Nevertheless, there was still a counter-argument. More than a week before the final, 130,000 copies of the match-day programme were printed and put on sale in bookstores all over the country. And they had Stephens, not Lovett, listed in Albion's troublesome right-wing role. Everton's line-up showed Roger Kenyon at no 10, although John Hurst staked his claim to a recall after jaundice by playing well against West Ham.

Highbury was a mudbath after torrential rain and Albion could have done without the sapping conditions that greeted them. The players' kit at the end was more in keeping with mid-January than mid-May and Ashman's virtual full-strength side had the extra discomfort of being well beaten, Doug Fraser's surging late run and shot bringing a consolation goal after Bobby Gould and

Frank McLintock had struck for the Gunners either side of the interval.

It wouldn't have been an Albion match of the time without injury scares. Graham Williams needed treatment on his return from knee trouble and, more worryingly, Graham Lovett was caught on the shin by a high tackle from Peter Storey. "I played on in the second half but the wound opened up again and Alan Ashman told me to go in on the Sunday," Lovett recalls.

"Such matters were normally left until the Monday and, when I arrived, Alan's car was already there and he was hovering around, asking the doctor whether the problem was long-term. In hindsight, I suppose that was a clear indication that he wanted me to play at Wembley. It was a clue I was going to be in, although I'm not sure I realised it at the time. I still had to get fit and, thankfully, the injury healed very quickly."

Lovett, who had started only seven League games all season and made three substitute appearances, was given one stitch in the wound and an injection to guard against possible infection. The scare had hit the one member of Albion's expectant playing staff who had already had more than his fair share of misfortune. But at least that's all it was: A scare.

Tony Brown takes the ball out of danger in the mudbath of Highbury, watched by (left to right) captain Graham Williams, Rick Sheppard and John Talbut.

Lovett hadn't been seen in the Cup 12 since going on as sub in the fourth-round replay win at Southampton but he was now very much in the frame. The big question was whether he had done enough to secure the right-wing slot and rebuff the challenges of Nick Krzywicki, Kenny Stephens, Asa Hartford and Dennis Clarke.

Comfortingly, Alan Ashman had options. Apart from Eddie Colquhoun, he had a full hand with which to plan for the challenge presented by Everton's big array of internationals and, with keeper John Osborne okay, he was able to issue an optimistic bulletin after a full-scale practice match in training early in the big week. "It's reassuring to see all the lads fit and well," he said. "It's great to be able to kick off Cup Final week with an injury-free squad."

With nine London-bound British Rail trains now filled by a total of 5,000 supporters, expectations were reaching fever pitch and another batch of 130,000 programmes were printed, this time carrying Graham Lovett's name at no 7 in the Albion side rather than Kenny Stephens. The final piece of the jigsaw was dropping into place.

Amid all the anticipation, a famous Baggies voice made his own plea to the players who carried the club's hopes. Ronnie Allen, scorer of the first two goals in Albion's 1954 Final victory over Preston, was the subject of a lengthy newspaper interview in the countdown to the game and urged his successors to savour the magical experience, win or lose.

"There's nothing quite like the FA Cup Final at Wembley in the life of a professional footballer," he wrote. "The atmosphere is terrific and so is the occasion. I would urge the Albion players to enjoy the whole 90 minutes because it will live with them for the rest of their lives and they may not get another chance. Many players at Wembley fall short of their true form because they are too nervous but I feel it's essential they enjoy it."

Allen's two-goal heroics 14 years earlier mirrored what W G Richardson did in the club's triumph over Birmingham in the 1931 Final. Now, pundits and supporters alike were wondering whether Jeff Astle could follow suit and net two of his own to put the glorious finishing touches to his feat of scoring in every round of the competition.

The FA Cup Final was not a social occasion to rival Ascot, Wimbledon or the Boat Race but it was, as one commentator called it at the time, a game of the people played for the people by the people. Although tickets even then were too prone to go to sources other than the fans of the finalist clubs, it was an event guaranteed to have tens of thousands converging on the capital.

'Up for the Cup' is how the mass day-out had become known, ever since Blackburn followers had flocked south for a Final in the 1880s and been described in the Pall Mall Gazette as 'a northern horde of uncouth garb and strange oaths' whose behaviour was likened to 'a tribe of cannibals let loose.' Albion v Everton in 1968 didn't attract quite the same colourful language but it was still a great occasion. And it wasn't only the players and paying supporters who were getting ready for it.

In liaison with manager Alan Ashman, club officials decided the squad's other halves were to be transported to London early on the Saturday morning and then taken on after the game to the luxurious Park Lane Hotel, where they would be joined by their menfolk and accommodated overnight following a banquet.

The players, with partners, had then been booked on the 11.45am train out of Euston on Sunday, ready for a 1.40pm arrival in New Street and an onward journey by open-top coach for the homecoming and a 2.30pm reception at West

Bromwich Town Hall, with or without the gleaming silverware Albion were so keen to get their hands on for the fifth time.

Even the biggest names in Ashman's team did not have superstar status and, unheard of today, no eyebrows were raised when the Express & Star printed an article on the players' better halves and named Springfield Crescent, West Bromwich, as the road where Laraine Astle lived with her famous husband. The squad lived in the local communities and blended in almost seamlessly.

Laraine was a regular Albion watcher, away as well as at home, although attendance had become more difficult in the month the Cup run started when three-year-old daughter Dorice found herself joined by a baby sister, Dawn. Mum treated herself to a new turquoise suit for Wembley, then convinced herself it was green and wouldn't wear it because it was considered unlucky.

Unlucky was a word that definitely applied to John Osborne's wife Jenny. He treated her to a new outfit ready for London, only for the couple to turn their backs on the purchase while they bought a newspaper in Birmingham's New Street. In the space of a few seconds, the bag and its contents disappeared from off the footpath by them - a rare case of the keeper's trusty hands not quite being trusty enough!

The shopstaff were alerted and, through friends in the media, Osborne offered the reward of a Cup Final ticket for the safe return of the garments. He didn't need to worry. They turned up safe when the woman who had taken the bag from beside the pushchair of the couple's daughter Suzanne, returned to the store and asked if she could have a different size! She was subsequently fined £10 and Mrs Osborne had her black sequined top and crepe skirt after all.

Such had been the demand for Wembley tickets that Heather Williams admitted to taking the phone off the hook at the home she shared with skipper Graham and their two children in Four Oaks, near Sutton Coldfield. "You can lose so many friends but people are ringing non-stop and asking if we have any spare tickets," she said.

John Talbut's wife Ena was another to use the team's progress to the Final as an excuse for adding to her wardrobe. The couple had three children at their home in Great Barr but that didn't stop the outlay on a nice navy and white number. The player's mother made a different kind of sacrifice. She was closing her fish and chip shop in Burnley for the day so she could be at Wembley!

Carol Hope, wife of Albion's main midfield creator, was also preparing to break with habit on May 18. The secretary regarded herself as something of a curse on the team and said: "They tend to lose when I go." But she added with a smile: "I'm going to risk it on Saturday!"

Alan Ashman's squad had long since been measured for and fitted with their special grey Wembley suits but the player and spouse arrangements seemed

straightforward compared with the preparations of lifelong Albion supporter Tony Willis from Tipton.

He had made his transport plans for the big day while the dust was still settling on the club's semi-final victory over Birmingham. Trouble was, he wasn't travelling in from the Black Country, but from the heart of Africa. The 29-year-old, who had been watching Albion with his two brothers since he was a toddler, was working as a mining engineer for the Anglo-American Copper Company 4,250 miles away in Zambia and had booked a flight that was due to touch down in London around midnight on the Friday night before the Final.

When he set about buying a ticket from The Hawthorns, though, he was told: "Sorry, we've sold out." Thankfully, his girlfriend was more fortunate in her enquiries. She worked in an office at which one of the staff had a spare ticket which she was able to purchase before cabling the good news half-way across the world.

A Dream Come True

You could write a book on Graham Lovett alone. After all, not many players are dubbed the new Duncan Edwards and then chopped down by a car crash that could have cost them their life. Fewer still bounce back from that sort of nightmare to gain an FA Cup winners' medal, only to come close to perishing for a second time in a heap of twisted metal.

Lovett's is a remarkable story of bravery and misfortune. He fought back on that second occasion as well, although he was never quite the player who had thrilled Hawthorns audiences in the mid-1960s. Then, England honours had seemed a certainty for the youngster - a far cry from the day when he was told he was too small to play for Birmingham schoolboys' side.

He was born near Birmingham City's ground and lived only a goal-kick from their training pitches at Sheldon, so it was natural that, awe-struck, he should watch them at work. Like England World Cup captain Bobby Moore, he modelled himself on Ray Barlow, who had finished his playing career at Blues. But it was Barlow's main club, Albion, who offered him his big breakthrough in the game.

After his initial knock-back, Lovett grew almost a foot. Albion were prepared to overlook his lack of inches because manager Jimmy Hagan felt he had an 'athletic frame that would develop.' Sure enough, he played for the club as an amateur, started the 1964-65 season in the third team and then turned out 11 times in the reserves.

But, at the age of only 17, he was given a shock Albion debut at home to Chelsea in December, 1964. It was only four weeks earlier that he had signed full-time. When kidded beforehand by senior Albion players that his chance was about to come, he demonstrated his shyness by hiding in the showers. And he was still so surprised at being called into Hagan's office the day before the match that he assumed it was for a ticking-off.

Lovett played against Chelsea at left-half in place of Terry Simpson, who had figured in the previous 62 games. He was detailed to mark no less a figure than Terry Venables, whose only two full England caps were won that very winter. The youngster was on £12 a week and, following the death of his father the previous year, had plans for his wages. "I want to help my Mum," he said.

He was immensely proud of his livelihood in the game but his growth spurt was not doing much for the family budget. "I hope I've stopped putting on the inches now because it's costing me a fortune in new suits!" he added. "I keep outgrowing them." He was a good-looking lad and cared about his appearance.

Debut-day was no fairytale as second-in-the-table Chelsea departed from The Hawthorns with a 2-0 win, George Graham scoring one of two goals Tommy Docherty's men plundered in the last 20 minutes. Lovett was replaced by Simpson for the following weekend's home draw against Manchester United but returned, again at no 6, for the defeat at Fulham a week later.

That was it for him for the season as Albion overcame a sticky mid-winter to finish 14th and it was in a 3-0 home win against West Ham, after he had figured in two hectic summer tours with the club to South America and New York, that he was next seen in League football.

This time, he stayed in the side, his tally of 38 appearances in the League, one in the FA Cup and eight in the League Cup making this his best season, although he still had the misfortune of being sidelined on the memorable February night Albion won the League Cup with a brilliant first-half blitz of West Ham in the Hawthorns (second) leg of the two-leg final.

He played in 21 of the first 26 games of the following season, including the away leg against DOS Utrecht in the club's first-ever competitive European tie, then, three weeks after reserve centre-half Danny Campbell had fractured his skull in a car accident in Manchester, came near-disaster on Christmas Eve, 1966.

Lovett suffered a blow-out on the M1 while on his way to take Christmas presents to his girlfriend in Essex and lay injured for 40 minutes before being attended by an ambulance crew. He was left with fractured vertebrae in his neck and partial paralysis.

"I was taken to Northampton General Hospital and put on traction," Lovett recalls. "My car had rolled over three times, gone up the bank and come to rest on the hard shoulder. Fortunately, it landed the right way up. Once I had been properly assessed, the general feeling was that my football career was over and the club surgeon told me as such.

"He said the only chance I had of playing again was if, when I felt a bit better, I had an operation to remove some bone from my hip and graft it to the neck. Even then, it was only 50-50 that I would recover for football purposes and there was always the outside chance that something might go wrong and I could be totally paralysed."

The operation, performed by honorary Albion surgeon Dr J H Kirkham, had been carried out only once in the previous ten years in West Bromwich and, on that earlier occasion, the patient had, indeed, suffered some paralysis. It was a big gamble.

For John Osborne, the Lovett tragedy was history repeated. The keeper had been given his first-team breakthrough as a Chesterfield player as a result of a car crash that cost team-mate Ralph Hunt his life and caused first-choice keeper

Graham Lovett, alongside Percy Freeman and Alan Merrick, manages a smile on the comeback trail from his appalling injuries.

Ron Powell leg injuries that prevented him playing again. Lovett faced a big battle to avoid going the same way as the favourite who preceded Osborne between the Saltergate posts.

The player, then only 19, was in Northampton General for several weeks and, ironically, one of his few excursions - under the strictest of supervision from the hospital's deputy superintendent - was to see Albion play and win an FA Cup third-round tie at Northampton in January, 1967. He watched from the directors' box and was lifted by a brief meeting with his team-mates in the dressing-room.

The bone graft was advised after the healing of the dislocated vertebrae had not gone as well as anticipated. "I quickly decided I would have the operation," Lovett added. "Paralysis was still a danger anyway if I tripped awkwardly. My first reaction was just to ensure I got better, with or without football. But as I improved and started walking about, albeit with some pain, I began to think I might make it back.

"I remember the old Albion keeper Jim Sanders was in the opposite ward having treatment for shrapnel in his leg and I was in hospital for several months. It was while I was in there watching the 1967 FA Cup Final between Tottenham and Chelsea that a friend of mine from Halesowen, Arthur Tildesley, came in and tried to cheer me up. He said: 'Never mind, you'll be playing at Wembley yourself next year!'"

Lovett could do nothing for three or four months after emerging from the theatre in West Bromwich, his neck immobilised by a collar. Then, with his rehabilitation under-way, the range of movement increased gradually over several painstaking weeks. He was back in third-team football early in 1967-68 and says: "I estimate I got back 95 per cent of the mobility in my neck.

"But it was a very long and painful road and I'm sure plenty of people thought I wouldn't make it. I had my doubts myself on occasions. Obviously, it was a dream what then happened because I had no idea at all what lay round the corner."

By coincidence, Lovett's comeback game was as a substitute for Clive Clark at home to Manchester City in December. It was against the same opponents at The Hawthorns the previous December that he had played the final game before his accident.

"Albion had already been to Wembley in my absence for the 1967 League Cup Final against QPR and I didn't really believe I could be so lucky as to make a good recovery and for the club to go to the FA Cup Final with me in with a chance of playing," he added. "That's just what happened, although I might have come to more harm after the semi-final.

"I lived among a lot of Birmingham fans and was nearly lynched by my mates when I went into my local, the Chestnut Tree in Sheldon, after we had beaten Blues. I had to remind them that it was nothing to do with me. I hadn't been on the pitch and wasn't even named as substitute!

"Seriously, it had obviously been a dreadful time for me and, as I had only ever been to Wembley for a schoolboy international, it was something else to go back there and be part of an FA Cup Final squad after all the problems I'd had. It was a wonderful experience that I'll never forget."

The Southport Spirit

They could have gone to Blackpool, Weston-Super-Mare or anywhere along the stretch of North Wales coast that Graham Williams knew well from his time as a young player for Rhyl Athletic. The fact that Albion, under two different managers in the late 1960s, chose Southport as their regular hideaway became hugely ironic in the latter stages of their glorious 1967-68 FA Cup run.

The bracing seaside town was a magnet for golfers with the championship links of Royal Birkdale bordered by the Ainsdale and Formby courses and only a couple of booming drives and an estuary away from another famous Open Championship venue, Royal Lytham and St Anne's. Southport's beach also later became a famous training ground for Red Rum before the Grand National winner's heroics down the A565 at Aintree.

But, for West Bromwich Albion's management and players to go there to plot the Cup exit of the might of Merseyside - first Liverpool and then Everton - was almost mischievous. Southport is, after all, only a few postcodes away from Anfield and Goodison Park and both clubs had players and fans living in the town. The resort also just happened to be home to Everton manager Harry Catterick.

Five times in just over a year, Albion had swapped the routine of Black Country life with the cleaner air of the Lancashire coast and, despite the separations from loved ones, the trips were a bit of a treat for the players. Probably more important than that, though, they had come to be seen as happy omens; a good-luck charm that the club dared not let go of.

Just as Jeff Astle wore the same outfit on every FA Cup match-day and John Osborne would always emerge last from the tunnel on to the pitch, so it became unthinkable that Alan Ashman's squad would spend the last few days before Cup-ties anywhere other than in the pleasant resort of Southport.

It had all started in the spring of 1967 when chairman Jim Gaunt, at Liverpool with the club's reserves, heard that the first team had been plunged deeper into relegation danger by losing 1-0 at home to Arsenal. Immediately, he rang his second-in-command Tommy Glidden and suggested the players be whisked away for a few days to recharge run-down batteries.

"I proposed Southport for a week and suggested the manager should put the emphasis on light training with plenty of golf and general relaxation," Gaunt said. "A meeting of the directors was called for the next day and the trip was agreed. After a couple of days, the tension began to lift and, in the next 11 games, we took 18 points and finished close to mid-table."

If the ploy worked then, it was certainly working in 1968 and, following a vigorous final training session on home soil, there was a spring in the squad's collective stride as a 14-man party climbed aboard and headed back up the M6 on the Tuesday before Wembley. Departure was accompanied by all the usual wisecracking, much of it from the mouth of Jeff Astle. But it also carried a tinge of sadness.

Asa Hartford, still five months short of his 18th birthday, had played three of the final four League games and allowed himself just a thought that he might have forced his way into the Wembley line-up. But, four seasons after Howard Kendall had become the youngest-ever FA Cup finalist at the age of 17 years 345 days, it wasn't to be. The rookie Scot, who would be 17 years 206 days old on the afternoon of the Everton game, was left behind.

John Osborne, Kenny Stephens and Dennis Clarke were the three players added to the 11 who had played at Arsenal, so there was no place either for Nick Krzywicki, who had played in the first meetings with both Colchester and Southampton at the start of the run and in the first leg of the three-match marathon against Liverpool. Keeper Rick Sheppard was included but only in case of emergency surrounding Osborne.

There wasn't a lot of hard work to do on the training ground. The side had just played an exhausting 14 games in a month and a half, so hours of physical exertion was not part of the itinerary. There was a lively run along windswept Ainsdale beach on the Wednesday but Southport that week was all about rest, keeping Wembley nerves at bay, a bit of sharpening-up and consolidating that famous Cup-fighting spirit.

"Fitness wasn't a big problem for the players, so training was nothing strenuous," recalls skipper Graham Williams. "We attended to the bonding things and everything was done together. There was a casino nearby for those who liked a bet and Jeff Astle was in his element because a lot of jockeys stayed with us at the Prince of Wales Hotel as a base for riding nearby.

"We were well aware that we were up in Everton and Liverpool country but we never had that much attention paid to us when we were out training, either on the beach or on a grass area near the promenade. We just got on with our work and made sure we remained as relaxed as possible. The last thing Alan Ashman wanted was for us, especially the younger lads in the squad, to become uptight."

The manager also organised a seven-a-side on the sands and declared himself happy with how his players looked. "I'm satisfied with how the lads are working in training," he said. "They have really been going at it." There was still time, though, for Jeff Astle to don his full all white match kit and practise his heading near the sea front for the benefit of the BBC cameras.

The Prince of Wales Hotel a couple of streets away from Southport's sea front - a key part of Albion's FA Cup strategy in 1967-68 when it became their regular getaway.

In Albion's midst was Dennis Shaw, then the chief sports writer of the Birmingham-based Evening Mail and the man assigned to cover the latter stages of the journey to Wembley. He, too, packed his bags each time Albion descended on Southport, increasingly confident that he was going to be reporting at close quarters on more West Midlands FA Cup success.

"I was a Villa fan and had been lucky enough to report on all their ties when they won the FA Cup in 1957," he said. "But that Albion side contained some terrific talent and were a good bunch who I liked a lot. They came together from various routes and had either been signed from here and there or had progressed through the Hawthorns ranks. But they were great entertainers and they scored tremendous goals.

"They also had this super togetherness and huge team spirit which meant they would do anything for each other. I didn't get close to any of them as friends but I spent a lot of time travelling in their company and grew very fond of them. They had a lot of what I would call men's men and they were a happy bunch, a good combination.

"I remember how much they loved playing cards. On one European trip, they had a hand going when we arrived at the hotel and they just sat down in the foyer to carry on playing at a table while the club officials attended to the

128

checking-in formalities. Italy, Holland, Spain...it didn't matter. They were more interested in taking a few bob off each other than looking at the sights, even though foreign travel was nothing like as commonplace as now.

"The Prince of Wales became recognised as Albion's lucky hotel. Going to Southport was not a special training thing, certainly not in the later rounds. It was just part of the package. If it was Cup week, off we would go to the seaside and Alan Ashman and Stuart Williams would make sure there was some fun as well as work. The time would pass quickly without anyone becoming uptight about matches.

"Near the hotel, there was a casino or nightclub called the Astoria, where I recall we all went over to watch a drag act one evening. The players would be allowed out for a beer early in the week but not at the end. As the matches approached, they had to settle for watching us going out! But we all got on well and you could tell the team spirit was terrific."

The selling of tickets for big matches was seen as a dressing-room perk at Wembley-bound clubs in those days, when wages in the game were much, much lower. The practice, now looked on a lot more disapprovingly, provides Dennis Shaw with one of his memories of Jeff Astle, who was later banned from receiving FA Cup Final tickets after admitting he made more than £200 through selling them.

"It was on the Thursday before one game," Shaw added. "Jeff saw me striding out across the road and shouted from his hotel window: 'Hey, youth! Will you spiv me some tickets?' He tore open a cigarette packet and wrote down his prices for me, and made sure I took it. That was Jeff, the life and soul of the group, a bit raucous and always very cheerful.

"Tony Brown was a big pal of his but quieter. John Kaye was a man of very few words, but something of a tough guy, like Graham Williams and Doug Fraser. They weren't cloggers but they were very physical when they had to be and the side had lots of resilience. Graham was the organiser and always very intimidating on the pitch. He was an inspirational leader.

"The John Kaye incident at Manchester City in the quarter-final was like the one when John Wile had to have his head bandaged in the semi-final at Highbury many years later. There was blood pouring everywhere and Kaye showed how brave and unflinching he was. He just carried on playing heroically and ignoring the pain he must have been in.

"Then there was John Osborne, who was very intelligent and immensely likeable but also very nervous. Strangely for a keeper, he often seemed to lack confidence. Before one FA Cup tie, I was in my room up in Southport and heard this thumping noise from the corridor. I rushed out to see what was happening and there was Ossie, in his training gear and with a cigarette on, walking along bouncing the ball. 'Just practising my handling, Dennis!' he shouted when he saw me."

It wasn't only the character of the players that impressed Shaw. He knew he was also watching a highly capable team who had a capacity to thrill. "They were a tremendous footballing side and great to watch," he added. "Bobby Hope could do many of the things Beckham can do, notably hit a pass without signalling it first. There was more space behind defences in those days and he was an expert at finding it.

"They had terrific skill through the side with Hope, who Bill Shankly always wanted to sign, Chippy Clark, Ian Collard and Graham Lovett. Then there were those two up front, Astle and Brown, if you can say Brown was a forward. It's probably difficult for younger fans to comprehend how good the pair were together but I would say they were better than Owen and Heskey. Put all the ingredients together and what more could you want?"

Dennis Shaw's friend and journalistic rival, Ray Matts of the Express & Star, has a fond memory of his own from the days leading up to Wembley - and an illustration of what an expert the players' gaffer was, or at least what an expert he appeared to be, at letting all the tension wash over him.

Alan Ashman was named Manager of the Month for April by a panel of sportswriters and seemed to be taking the pressure of Cup Final countdown in his stride. "While we were in Southport, he was invited to the TV studios in Manchester and he asked me to go along with him in the taxi for company while Stuart Williams remained with the players at the hotel," Matts recalls.

"Harry Catterick was also there and, after they had done their bit for Harry Carpenter and the Sportsnight cameras, Catterick said he would give Alan a lift back as he lived in Southport. I sat in the back of the car and was amazed to see and hear the two of them discussing every possible facet of the game of football, yet not once mention the FA Cup Final!

"It was a real education hearing them discussing the state of the sport at such length and dissecting every aspect of it. But the word Wembley wasn't uttered and, when we pulled up outside the Prince of Wales Hotel, they just said to each other: 'Right, see you on Saturday.' And that was it.

"As the local reporter, I was very close to the Albion camp and used to get a lot of mickey-taking from the players when other journalists called the hotel from back in the West Midlands or London. The tanoy would ask for Mr Alan Ashman to go to the phone in reception. If he was unavailable, a call for Mr Stuart Williams would follow a few seconds later. And, if he wasn't around either, the third message would be for Mr Ray Matts!

"I would pass on a few details about injuries and such like to the reporters, then get an awful lot of stick from the players about being seen as part of the management team! But it was wonderful to be trusted enough to be on the inside of it all and they were really great times.

"The squad were like a brotherhood. You had the older ones like Graham Williams, who was the organiser of everything, John Kaye and John Talbut. The two Johns didn't say a lot but were very close and, as good northern lads do, just had the knack of bringing someone down a peg or two when necessary with a well-chosen remark.

"Bobby Hope and Doug Fraser were good mates as fellow Scots, Bobby quieter and much more serious, and tremendously gifted on the field. Then there was John Osborne, who was like the lovable, dopey one. He was always injured and in need of a psychological crutch from the management or the other players. He had a ritual of taping two fingers together before every match because of an arthritic condition and the lads often felt like saying: 'Ossie, don't bother playing today. We'll call the ambulance now!'

"Clive Clark was also a bit of a worrier, as well as being a loner at times, while Graham Lovett, Ian Collard, Dennis Clarke, Nick Krzywicki, Kenny Stephens and Rick Sheppard were the younger ones who stuck together and were in and out of the side.

"Then there were Tony Brown and Jeff Astle - the two inseparable scamps and similar in personality to Doug Fraser. Jeff got away with being Jeff. He had bad matches but, when he was on his game and he knew he had the beating of the centre-half, he was the absolute business.

"There's a famous story from that time of how Alan Ashman went in to give a team-talk one Saturday afternoon, found Jeff and a few other players in front of the TV watching a race and wasn't too pleased about not getting their proper attention. As a result, there was no team talk but Jeff repaid him by going out and scoring a hat-trick.

"They were an incredibly 'together' bunch of blokes. You can't buy team spirit. It's either there or it isn't and those players just had it in abundance. Alan Ashman had had the good sense not to interfere with his squad too much when he took over and they just hit it off for him.

"I don't think they realised how good a team they were. Tony Brown could have gone into any team and done well. Jeff Astle was as good a traditional centre-forward as there was around and the best manager of the day reckoned Bobby Hope could cross the ball on to a sixpence. Then they had a current Welsh international as skipper who would have found a place in most teams.

"Clive Clark was quick and a great crosser of the ball, as well as a prolific goalscorer, the two centre-halves John Talbut and John Kaye were rock-solid. And Doug Fraser was a sound player and a Scottish cap. They were a terrific team. Their only problem was that they remained inconsistent and you could

Working out on the Southport beach under the supervision of Stuart Williams are (from left) Brown, Talbut (near camera), Sheppard, Clark, Osborne, Stephens, Lovett, Collard, Astle, Williams, Fraser (near camera), Kaye and Hope.

never really envisage them challenging for the League Championship."

There may have been great trust in the local media but Ashman saw fit to lay down a few ground rules for Cup Final week: No interviews without permission and no stunt pictures. Albion had other Pressmen in their midst at times, some from the national sector, and skipper Graham Williams would usually act as the go-between.

"We would sometimes have a lad called Ken Jones with us," Williams said. "He was the cousin of the former Tottenham and Wales winger Cliff Jones. I used to see him at international games and he would give Albion some real stick. He would slag us off and keep forecasting we would lose, so, with each round that went by, I told him to carry on!

"Then there was Peter Batt, who once fell asleep in his biryani at a restaurant, and the local guys Bob Blackburn, Jeff Farmer, Ray Matts and Dennis Shaw. Matts was a decent gambler, so was Farmer, who was also in charge of a football team called the Flower Pot, who a few of the lads would go and watch play. He was a keen cards player and would play Jeff Astle and Tony Brown, who would take the money and take the mickey in equal quantities!

132

"And that was a big part of the trips to Southport. It was all about keeping relaxed and bonding with each other. We had a fantastic team spirit and being together so much helped. Our only star was Jeff, who no-one would ever have a go at because it was often his goals that earned us some bonus! And it was because of him that training and bus journeys never dragged. He was just so funny."

Such was the mood among the players that full-back Doug Fraser revealed in an interview from the club's Cup Final hideaway: "The atmosphere here has been so relaxing that I really haven't thought that much about the game." And his fellow Scot Bobby Hope revealed recently that other matters were often on the players' minds.

"Once when we were up at Southport, the Grand National meeting was on at Aintree and a jockey called Tony Murray was staying at the Prince of Wales," he said. "He gave us what he insisted was a red-hot tip but advised us that we would have to get our money on it first thing the next morning because the price was about to come down.

"Fortunately, our coach driver enjoyed a flutter as well, so six or seven of us persuaded him to take us up to the course on the bus after breakfast to lay our bets. We did - and the horse won. But we probably had another dozen 'red-hot' tips later on that came nowhere and we soon realised that jockeys are the worst tipsters in the world!"

Back with football issues, it had been an extraordinary 12 months for Alan Ashman. When the big clash with Everton came round, it was a year to the day since Albion's board had met him at a football writers' dinner in London the night before the Spurs v Chelsea FA Cup Final and made it very clear he was their choice as successor to Jimmy Hagan.

Maybe Ashman's own relaxed state of mind was a reflection of the trust he had in his players to get the job done and the game won. He developed a priceless camaraderie and one-for-all, all-for-one mentality that meant any crisis could be overcome. And there had certainly been a few crises before the club were able to book a place in their tenth FA Cup Final.

Graham Williams, who still dishes out the orders and organises the players' reunions, typified the determination to fight battles as a team. He said: "In the days when we would play the same club in successive midweeks early in the season, Doug Fraser and I once had a battering off Trevor Hockey in a match at Newcastle.

"As we were walking off at the end, Doug grabbed him by the back of the hair and told him how much he was looking forward to seeing him the next week at The Hawthorns. In the second match, we set about getting even with him and closed in when there was a loose ball. Unfortunately, Trevor stepped aside and the two of us collided. I broke Doug's nose and he split my lip so badly that I still have the scar!

"It backfired on us on that occasion but that togertherness was always there. We would do anything for one another and the closeness and comradeship in the squad were a big factor behind our success. We would go out together and enjoy each other's company, so much so that we often didn't want to go home from training. Many's the time we would stage an England v Celts five-a-side, a head-tennis game or a table tennis competition among us in the afternoon.

"There were all these different personalities in the mixer but Alan Ashman brought them together for the common good. We had such respect for him because he treated us right and we would never have wanted to let him down in any way.

"John Kaye and John Talbut were like brothers and lived near each other in Great Barr. Big T had a short fuse at times and Yorky would have to control him. They would go out for a pint at the Scott Arms a bit closer to a game than most of us would and Alan just used to tell them: 'I know you have a drink, but just have the one.' They did.

"Ossie always let you know he had injuries and you had to treat him tenderly at times before he went out to play. You had to look after him. I don't know where he got his confidence from because he was always terribly nervous before matches. But, when he got the bit between his teeth, he used to tell us: 'Don't worry, lads, they won't score today.' And, usually, when he was in that mood, they didn't."

It was all about the blend. Osborne, Kaye, Astle and Clark had come from the lower divisions, Fraser and Hope from Scotland, Talbut from top-flight rivals Burnley and Williams, Brown, Lovett, Collard and Clarke from the club's junior teams. But they mixed brilliantly, on the field and off it.

They could easily have scattered during the turbulent Jimmy Hagan reign because the man whose brilliant talent-spotting network had taken most of them to The Hawthorns was guilty of the man-management failings that had players queuing up to leave in 1966-67. Happily, they stayed and the more laid-back Alan Ashman was able to get the very best out of them.

"Alan was great to work for because you knew where you stood with him," says John Kaye. "He was dead straight with us. There was no stabbing in the back. He was good at the banter and the players liked that. He used to encourage it and it was tremendous fun, especially when Jeff was around. But, if anyone needed any help, with their football or otherwise, there were plenty of people who were willing to lend a hand."

It was in Southport on the Wednesday afternoon that Ashman, privately at least, named his 11 for the twin towers. Ten of his side had been certain of inclusion and the last place, the no 7 shirt, went to Graham Lovett, who won the vote ahead of Kenny Stephens and, to a lesser extent, Dennis Clarke.

Stephens and stand-by keeper Rick Sheppard were taken on one side by the manager and let down as gently as possible while Clarke's dissatisfaction at his general lack of opportunities led to further discussions about his future during the stay in Southport, several weeks on from when he had had a transfer request thrown out.

Stephens' disappointment can hardly be overestimated but Clarke's was at least tempered by the fact that he was named as substitute. Not that subs ever got on in FA Cup Finals - or did they?

On the other side of the coin, the naming of the team was a proud moment for 20-year-old Lovett. It was confirmation that he had won the battle to reassert himself following career-threatening injuries. Now, all he had to do was contain his excitement and keep the lid on the selection for a few more hours.

"I remember one of the journalists following me into the gents before the team had been made public," he recalled. "He was looking for a clue as to the line-up and perhaps thought he would get one from me, a youngster who was less versed in the need for all this secrecy. He said 'Congratulations on your selection.' I was within a split-second of saying something to give the game away, then remembered what Alan had ordered, so I said nothing."

It was on the Thursday - a day when Albion had a light session near the sea front - that the football world learned of their line-up. And Lovett was able to speak at last of his delight: "It's difficult to believe that, only last summer, I was lying in hospital after a big operation on my neck after watching Albion play QPR in the League Cup Final from my ward.

"Now, a year on, I'm playing at Wembley myself and I can hardly believe it. It's wonderful. People said the injuries would ruin my career and there were times when the going was very tough. I've worked very hard to recover but now it all seems worthwhile.

"I have been waiting all week to hear if I was playing but I hadn't really dreamt I was in with a chance until the last few days. Naturally, I hoped I would be selected after playing at outside-right against Arsenal. But the conditions weren't good and I didn't have the best of matches. The guessing game has been going on here all week, with Kenny Stephens, Dennis Clarke and myself looking for clues.

"I normally share a room with Dick Sheppard but, when we booked in at the hotel here, I was put in with Ian Collard instead. That made me think I might be the lucky one. It seemed to be in my favour that I was with one of the team rather than the reserve goalkeeper.

"When the gaffer called a meeting to tell us the team, it was agonising as he went through the team name by name. When he got to outside-right, there was a long pause before he said 'Graham Lovett.' I can't describe the feeling. The room began to spin because I couldn't believe it. It's fabulous news for me."

Skipper Graham Williams still recognises the closeness of the battle for the right-wing role. "It was the only position that was in any doubt," he says. "Kenny Stephens had played well and had terrific skills that enabled him to go past defenders. But he was the quietest lad I ever met and spent a lot of his time reading the Sporting Life. He wouldn't say a thing. To me, he lacked ambition and could have gone on to do much better in the game.

"Graham Lovett was staking a strong claim and I think he got the nod because he was seen as better equipped to stop Ray Wilson getting forward. We were concerned about the overlaps from their left-back and, with the height of Joe Royle in their attack, obviously Everton were dangerous if a lot of crosses came into our penalty area.

"Graham was a terrific prospect in his younger years and could have played for England, only for his life to be turned upside down by those car crashes. He had various bits and pieces pinned in his body and I remember us saying we hoped it didn't rain at Wembley because, with all those nuts and bolts, there was a chance of him rusting up!"

Lovett's delight was mirrored at home - and in hospital. His mother Lucy, who was to settle for watching the Cup Final on TV, said: "I feel too full to say a lot but I'm very glad for him. I honestly didn't think he would play football again when he was in hospital in Northampton.

"Then, when he was told he might have a chance if he had the bone graft, I was very frightened. I told him not to have it and to forget about playing. I said I wouldn't care if he never kicked another ball as long as he was okay. But he told me football was his life and, if the operation gave him a chance of playing again, he would have it."

After the Lovett family, the happiest man at his Wembley selection was the surgeon who saved his playing career, Dr J H Kirkham. "It's a wonderful achievement of Graham's to have come back so well from all those injuries," he said. "It's entirely down to his own hard work and keenness. Most people would have lost their nerve after that accident but Graham worked hard to get himself back to fitness."

Nick Krzywicki's challenge for a Wembley place had petered out amid some anti-climax. He had been the other contender for the wide-right role, although a substitute's outing in the penultimate League game at Sunderland a fortnight earlier had been one of only two League appearances handed to him in the final three and a half months of the season.

"It was disappointing to play in a few of the ties and miss out on the Final," the winger said recently. "I hadn't played that many of the League games in the spring but nor had Graham Lovett because of his accident. I then thought I might have a chance as substitute but Alan Ashman opted for defensive cover with Dennis Clarke.

"I ended up going down to Wembley on the train with Ray Fairfax and sitting with Asa Hartford, Laraine Astle and Irene Brown at the game. It was still a great day and I remember I was absolutely hoarse at the end of it!"

There is no truth in the rumour, although it has become a good story to tell, that Alan Ashman made his choice only in the final hour before kick-off when the team-sheet was being filled in. In the presence of a waiting official, he is alleged to have painstakingly spelled out the names of all his players from one to six and then encountered problems. "K-r-i-z, no! K-r-y-z-w-y....oh, sod it, put Lovett down instead."

"Alan himself enjoyed telling that one over the years because that was his dry sense of humour," Lovett added. "But he had been keen that we knew the line-up early. I'm told they had two sets of programmes issued for the Final, one with me at outside-right and one with Kenny Stephens in. That's how close the choice was, so I was lucky to be picked. I think I got the nod because I was a more defensive type of player than Kenny and there was a need to keep an eye on Ray Wilson. We knew we had to stop the supply to Joe Royle in the air.

Jeff Astle demonstrates, by firing a cameraman's hat into the net on the Friday afternoon tour of Wembley, that he has observed manager Alan Ashman's orders not to pose for any more stunt photographs! Picture courtesy of Associated Newspapers.

"When my selection was confirmed to me, I expressed sympathy to Kenny Stephens. He had played well in the semi-final and must have thought he had a chance for Wembley. I was pally with him and Nicky Krzywicki because we were all the same age, although my best friend and my regular room-mate was Dick Sheppard.

"Unfortunately, only 11 players could be named in the starting line-up and one player's delight is another's disappointment. With all the health and fitness problems I had been through, nobody had to tell me how hard it must have been for the lads who just missed out on selection."

Journalists close to the Everton camp were having a hectic time. They were not only busy predicting the team Harry Catterick would name but also penning a story that had nothing to do with the players. Out of the blue, Liverpool police announced that thousands of forged Cup Final tickets had been printed and were on sale in pubs frequented by Everton fans.

They were by no means counterfeit masterpieces and the differences with the real thing were said to be 'so obvious to the trained eye that they will not get past the turnstiles.' But their presence on the market didn't stop unknowing supporters getting their fingers burned in a big way.

The forgeries reflected the huge clamour to be at the game and Labour's Eric Heffer, MP for the Merseyside constituency of Walton, wrote to Minister for Sport Denis Howell demanding that more tickets be sent to the two finalists. Everton had 18,000 season ticket holders and a Wembley allocation of only 16,000. As ever, impassionate watchers - fans of neither one club nor the other - would fill a lot of seats.

Albion chairman Jim Gaunt agreed with the sentiment and apologised to the many supporters who had been unsuccessful in their ticket applications to The Hawthorns. Like many regimes before and after, the two clubs' boards had not been able to squeeze a gallon into a pint pot, although there was one happy tale amid all the disappointment.

Fifteen-year-old Kingstanding schoolboy David Hill had admitted defeat in his bid to go to the game when, out of the blue, an anonymous fan sent him his own 10s (50p) ticket for the West enclosure. Unable to go himself, he had been stirred into the heart-warming gesture by the sight of a published letter in which Mr Hill Snr had bemoaned his son's misfortune.

David had seen every game in the Cup run (apart from Colchester away when he had had a heavy cold) and not missed a home game for three years, yet was convinced he was missing out on an unforgettable trip to Wembley. "It's the best present I could have had," he beamed after opening his post. And his match forecast: Albion 1 Everton 0, thanks to a goal by Astle!

Everton were behind Albion in naming their team - possibly because John

Hurst had been having daily checks from the Goodison doctor following his jaundice - but ahead of them in setting off for London. While their opponents were still chewing over Wembley tactics in 'Toffee country' on the Thursday, the Merseysiders had a final two-hour work-out at their Bellefield training headquarters and then headed south.

The team travelled on a train also well populated by fans determined to make a long weekend of it and were to stay at the same Surrey hotel that had served as their base before their 1966 Cup Final triumph over Sheffield Wednesday. Croquet was soon on the activity list for John Morrissey and reserve Sandy Brown but, surprisingly, manager Harry Catterick saw fit to put his players through a 20-minute cross-country run as well over a nearby golf course.

Albion's work was shorter and sharper, and they were looking forward to seeing Wembley's immaculate acres. They had played on a shocker of a pitch at Highbury the previous Saturday and were pleased to hear Percy Young, head groundsman at the national stadium for 30 years, say his pride and joy was 'in fine shape, a little yielding.'

Alan Ashman was carefully pacing the wind-down of his preparations and said on the Friday: "Certain aspects of the game will be discussed tonight but the important meeting will be the one in the hotel tomorrow morning. There's no tension among the players. They have had plenty of relaxation this week as well as work and everything has gone to plan."

Then came the fond farewells at the Prince of Wales Hotel before Albion headed south for an eve-of-Final look at the stadium prior to check-in at the Henley Hall Hotel, London. The biggest day of their lives was only hours away. The men who had grown up together as footballers were ready to go. The week had been largely restful but they had shown over and over again that they were prepared to put in an extra shift if necessary.

After their dramatic and sometimes traumatic Cup journey via Colchester, Southampton, Portsmouth, Liverpool, Manchester and Birmingham, it was next stop the twin towers. They had had some laughs up in Southport, now it was down to London. All for one and one for all; a group of down-to-earth blokes desperate to win for themselves and win for each other.

In a newspaper column in a countdown to the Final, John Kaye referred to his club colleagues as 'the best mates in the world.' With the big match now almost upon them, they were happy to leave their Southport hideaway behind for the last time. They couldn't wait to step into the full glare of the Wembley spotlight and depart it in triumph.

Final Preparations

Bill Lawry had just arrived in England to lead the 24th party of touring Australian cricketers, Colin Cowdrey had taken 127 off Somerset's attack at Gravesend, and Ipswich had won the Second Division title, to be accompanied into the top flight by QPR. Further afield, Juventus were just about to smash the world transfer record and splash out £400,000 on Pietro Anastasi from Varese.

The front pages in that mid-May week in 1968 made grim reading. The United States had suffered their worst week so far in the Vietnam War, with 562 deaths, and the pound had dropped by 17 points against the dollar to a new record low of $2.3854. But some things were familiar. The Duke of Edinburgh admitted he 'should have kept his trap shut' after criticising Australia's Chief Justice Sir Garfield Barwick in Sydney.

In showbiz, it had just been announced that Noele Gordon was leaving Crossroads. Among the other big programmes of the day were Z Cars, The Virginian (at the curious time of 7.06pm on Wednesday night), Moira Anderson Sings, Double Your Money and, for younger viewers, Magic Roundabout.

In the job market, the Royal Insurance announced in an advert that they would pay £520 to the successful applicant in their hunt for an underwriter and sales assessor. Once he or she had been installed for a couple of years, perhaps they would look for property.....a three-bedroom McLean house in the Black Country was going for £5,650.

Life operated on a different set of figures in the late 1960s and the dizziest Albion's players became was for youngsters Ian Collard and Dennis Clarke to muse over whether they would buy a TR6 or TR7 if they became FA Cup winners.

The period three and a half decades ago in which West Bromwich Albion last went to the final stage of the competition was an exciting time for English football. Thanks to an odd-goal semi-final success over Dundee, Leeds were through to a two-leg showdown with Ferencvaros in the last phase of the UEFA Cup's forerunner, the Inter Cities Fairs Cup, and Manchester United - pipped to the League title by Manchester City a few days earlier - drew 3-3 at the Bernabeau Stadium to overcome mighty Real Madrid on aggregate and reach a Wembley showdown with Benfica in the European Cup.

At the same time, the nation was eagerly anticipating Saturday, May 18, West Bromwich Albion v Everton and the 87th staging of the FA Cup Final. Goals were guaranteed. A feast of football was promised and fans of both clubs, as well as independent observers, were talking of a classic in the making for the masses to enjoy. It seemed utterly reasonable to be predicting a Final that would rival the Baggies' thrilling 3-2 win over Preston 14 years earlier.

No less an authority than Ronnie Allen - the two-goal hero of that 1954 triumph - forecast: "This could be a soccer showpiece." And the facts supported the optimism of a man then mid-way between his service as a much-revered forward in the club's colours and the first of his two stints as their manager.

Albion had finished eighth in the First Division, their haul of 46 points from 42 games (in the days of two points for a win) being built on the scoring of 75 goals - 1.785 per match. The fact Alan Ashman's side had also conceded 62 underlined why they were such great crowd-pleasers, although that latter tally was the club's lowest for four years and their second lowest for eight.

The facts still showed, though, what an uphill task they faced. Everton had finished three places and six points higher than them in the table and had an abundance of attacking riches. Not that their defence were to be sniffed at. The club's concession of only 40 goals made them the joint meanest side in the division along with Liverpool.

Everton were one of the four clubs who had been busy hogging English football's two main honours in the 1960s. The quartet of Manchester United, Tottenham and the two Mersey rivals had, between them, accounted for 12 of the previous 15 winnings of the League title and FA Cup, with only 1968 League champions Manchester City, 1964 FA Cup winners West Ham and 1962 League champions Ipswich interrupting the monopoly.

Albion had dominated the less celebrated League Cup for two years but had not made the slightest inroads into this major stranglehold, what with their FA Cup failings over the previous three seasons and their successive League finishes since 1961 of 10th, 9th, 14th, 10th, 14th, 6th, 13th and 8th. Now, if they were to get their hands on the big knockout prize, they had to take the scalp of the 1966 FA Cup winners and 1963 League champions.

Nationally, they still had a bit of an image problem. Their attendances remained modest and there was a long-held theory that players like Jeff Astle, Bobby Hope, Doug Fraser and Tony Brown would have played for their countries long before - and been considerably better paid! - had they been with clubs that were perceived as more glamorous.

Despite the justifiable hang-ups around The Hawthorns, though, Albion were a well-liked side. One columnist described them as 'carrying a touch of madness about them.' And he added: 'They have a vulnerability combined with thrilling counter-attacking and moments of inspiration.'

Alan Ashman was the man charged with the responsibility of keeping the goals coming at one end and stemming the flow at the other - a balancing act he appeared to have achieved with his emergency switch of front-runner John

Kaye to a defensive role alongside centre-half John Talbut, his close pal.

Kaye had started with Goole Town on £3 a week at the age of 17 and went on to play 77 League games during three and a half years with Scunthorpe United. Now, glory beckoned on the biggest domestic stage of all if Albion could come through one final test on a Cup run dogged by problems.

"We had had a settled side earlier in the season," he recalls. "I was playing in my old position up front and was happy that I was playing okay even though I wasn't scoring that many. I thought I was helping make a few for others by taking defenders out of the way and remember telling one centre-half who had come a long way out of defence with me that he should have been in the area marking Jeff because I wasn't going to score from where I was!

"I assumed I would be playing as a forward for the rest of the season, then the injuries came along. We had a lot of fitness problems in a short space of time but the one that most affected me was when poor Eddie Colquhoun badly tore his ankle ligaments up at Newcastle and I was sent back into defence. Fortunately, it didn't turn out to be a big hardship for me.

"I was big pals with John Talbut anyway and we had a good understanding. Our wives were friendly as well and we got on fine on the pitch. John would attack the first ball and I would play as sweeper. I was seen as the one who could read the game better and pick up a lot of the loose balls, whether John had won them or not. He was excellent in the air and I grew to enjoy the position more than up front because we were doing well."

Kaye, who had scored 23 goals in the 1965-66 campaign that elevated him into Alf Ramsey's World Cup 40 but, alas, not his final 22, had an extra little incentive to win at Wembley. Not only did he love the sense of fun he felt matches against Merseyside clubs always generated, he was also close to one or two members of the Goodison Park dressing-room.

On various England and Football League representative side get-togethers, he often roomed with Ray Wilson and Alan Ball and rated the latter above all others in the English game. Now, he was promising to put the clamp on them at Wembley, although he had already broken one promise during the countdown to the Final.

Superstition had decreed that he would not visit the barber's again until the Cup run was over but he was forced to go back on his word when he felt his hair would look a mess on television and was even in danger of getting in his eyes!

Away from such trivia, the forged ticket scandal was to have miserable consequences. One fan, Edward Ralph of Merseyside, was pictured in the national papers after paying £7 10s for a ticket he soon found to be forged. Even supporters who discovered they had become victims of a cruel con trick had not necessarily been put off travelling, though, and there was a danger of crushing when angry fans at Gate G Entrance 64 were turned away in their dozens.

Two men, rather than one, had been posted on each turnstile and Wembley Press Officer Len Went said: "There were only 1,800 genuine tickets for this block but I've seen some numbered over 5,000." Clearly, it had been a good time for the touts. In Liverpool, they were asking £8 for 10s (50p) tickets - and getting it. Prices were a bit lower in West Bromwich but standing tickets costing 22s 6d (about £1.12) and 45s (£2.25) were moving for £10 and £20.

Some estimates put the number of Everton supporters on the move on Cup Final day

Sick as a parrot.....Everton fan Edward Ralph, £7.50 poorer and the holder of a forged ticket.

at 30,000 - almost twice the number of their official ticket allocation - and one observer said: "There could be as many people outside the ground as in it."

The Final had generated record gate receipts of £110,000 but there were no transport hassles or forgery worries for 100 West Midlands pensioners. Thanks to an admirable gesture from radio and TV dealers Collis of the Midlands, they were taken to watch the game in colour at Wolverhampton's Bradmore Hotel.

Everton were bidding to lift the Cup for the second time in three years and for the fourth occasion in their 89-year history. They were in their sixth Final, having lost against Wolverhampton Wanderers (1893), Aston Villa (1897) and Sheffield Wednesday (1907) and beaten Newcastle United (1906), Manchester City (1933) and Sheffield Wednesday (1966).

Their path to the Final had contained none of the stress and little of the drama that had accompanied Albion's journey. They had not needed a single replay despite being drawn away three times out of four, and had conceded only one goal. They had endured but 450 minutes of playing time compared with their opponents' 840! That's the small difference of four and a bit matches.

Alan Ashman's side, having played only three of their nine pre-Wembley FA Cup games at The Hawthorns, had beaten taken to replays in three rounds, to extra-time in one of them, and had literally given blood to stay alive in the competition. Put another way, Everton might be said to have cruised first-class while Albion had been busy dodging the slings and arrows, their bandwagon finding plenty of potholes en route!

The cast-lists did not make comfortable reading either for those of a navy blue and white striped persuasion. The respective squad strengths were very much in the Merseysiders' favour. They had three current England stars in their side in majestic centre-half Brian Labone (on his way to a final haul of 26 full caps), midfield firebrand Alan Ball (destined to finish with 72) and his fellow World Cup winner Ray Wilson (who was to play 63 games for his country).

In addition, keeper Gordon West would soon play three England matches, Tommy Wright 11, Colin Harvey one and Joe Royle six. Graham Williams was the only regular international from Albion's Cup squad and his playing days were nearly over, although Doug Fraser and Bobby Hope were each shortly set to represent Scotland and Tony Brown and Jeff Astle were to win one and five England caps respectively.

Everton were also a club of considerable means. They had made West England's costliest goalkeeper when they handed Blackpool £27,500 for him, they had paid a record fee for a wing-half when recruiting Howard Kendall for £80,000 from Preston and they had smashed the record fee for a deal between two British clubs when their £110,000 cheque tempted Blackpool to part with Alan Ball. Other milestone deals had earlier hauled in Fred Pickering and Tony Kay - players who had by now moved on.

Ray Wilson, no relation to the Scottish-born Albion defender of the same name, was reputed to be Europe's best left-back, although he was 33 at the time of the Final. He and Ball had already won World Cup winners' medals with England, Kendall was so mature as to have played in the 1964 FA Cup Final for Preston at 17 and centre-forward Royle had been blooded in first-team football at the tender age of 16 years 282 days.

At the helm was Harry Catterick, who had been chaired from Wembley in 1965-66 in recognition of masterminding Everton's 3-2 FA Cup Final triumph over his former club Sheffield Wednesday from two goals down. The former four-handicap golfer had been in charge at Goodison Park since 1961 when taking over from Johnny Carey. And he had as his no 2, of course, Wilf Dixon, who had been a coach at Albion in the early 1960s.

The individual parts were convincing and the sum of them was even more formidable. No wonder Everton were 5-4 favourites. That season, they had beaten Albion 2-1 at Goodison Park in the October before embarrassing their Cup Final opponents to the tune of 6-2 at The Hawthorns on a March afternoon on which they fielded ten of the 11 players, Colin Harvey apart, who were likely to play at Wembley.

All told, they had won three of the previous four meetings of the clubs and lost only once in five clashes - a 1-0 defeat attended by England boss Sir Alf Ramsey in the West Midlands in January, 1967. But, despite having Labone in the peak of his form, they did lack one commodity their opponents had - Jeff Astle, the man the centre-half had the unenviable task of marking.

Astle had already finished the 1967-68 League campaign with 26 goals, a haul that included an early-season hat-trick at home to Sheffield United as well as those trebles against Manchester United and West Ham in a memorable three-night period in the spring.

"This has undoubtedly been my best ever season," he said a couple of days before the Final. "The team have been playing well and goals just seem to have come my way. I love to score but I owe a lot to Bobby Hope, whose pinpoint crosses have led to many of my goals. It just proves how one player's success depends on the work of his team-mates.

"I can't wait to get to Wembley. When I made my first visit there as a player for last year's League Cup Final, the fans gave us a fantastic reception when we walked out. I don't normally suffer from nerves because I'm more of a joker and nothing gets me down. But I think I'll be scared stiff as we come up the tunnel on Saturday and see and hear all the fans."

Surprisingly, Albion were seen as favourites by Don Revie, manager of the feared Leeds side who lost to Everton in the semi-final. Along with Stan Cullis, the other beaten manager from the last-four stage, Revie had been chosen for TV analyst duty and said: "I fancy Albion. I saw their replays against Liverpool and they look a great side. They can produce 15 minutes of superb attacking and take two goals off you in that time.

"It looks to me as though they have also tightened up their defence. Everton are a fine team and, defensively, they give nothing away. But Albion have a good enough attack to break through. In the semi-final, we played badly and didn't deserve to win. Everton didn't play much better but had one break with a penalty. On what I have seen, it's definitely Albion for me."

For the Cup Final, the Midlanders were staying in the same hotel that the England team used and had already won the toss for the privilege of using the spacious 'home' changing area occupied by Alf Ramsey's World Cup heroes two summers earlier. But Everton, having found themselves in the 'away' dressing-room, knew there would have to be a big surprise on the field if the FA Cup was to be taken back to the Black Country.

Albion had a shock result to inspire them the night before. While some of their players were holed up in their hotel and others, including Astle, took the opportunity to watch the Harlem Globetrotters basketball team on a visit to London, a strong England side lost 4-1 at Highbury to a Young England side for whom only centre-forward Martin Chivers went on to become a regular in the full team.

Back at the team's headquarters, there was more going on than the usual Friday-night-away activities like snooker and watching films. Although Alan Ashman had drawn a line under the chasing of perks by his players, they had already had some commercial success and several of the senior men had an urgent task to attend to in order to secure a useful bonus.

"There weren't that many financial spin-offs in those days and our build-up wasn't over-complicated by money matters," recalls skipper Graham Williams. "But John Osborne had been busy writing loads of letters and succeeded in getting us £500 in the kitty as a result of a deal with the Milk Marketing Board.

"Then there was Adidas's part in promoting the Final. They were putting money in and the players were expected to wear their boots in return. But the lads wanted to stick with their usual Puma footwear, so there we were the night before the match painting out the Puma logo and putting the three Adidas stripes on all the boots so as not to cause any offence!

"Another £25 was being paid for Stuart Williams to carry his magic sponge and other bits and pieces in an Adidas bag and we spent a few minutes working out the camera angles to make sure there was maximum exposure on TV!"

Williams had led Albion out against QPR in the 1966-67 League Cup Final, as well as in both legs against West Ham in the last two-legged final the year before. With one brilliant win and one hugely embarrassing defeat, he now had the opportunity to tip the scales back the right way.

"Having lost against QPR, it was a chance to go back and put things right," he says. "And this was a very big game for me. My family were Evertonians, in particular my father, who was a big fan and mad about Dixie Dean and Dave Hickson. He used to take me to Dixie's pub in Cheshire and make me wait outside while he pored over all the medals and famous pictures on the walls."

Williams' wife Heather had also been brought up in a neighbourhood where blue and white shirts - not the striped variety - were worn. And he added: "Living where I did, Everton games at The Hawthorns were the only ones that I was ever asked for tickets for. When Alan Ball scored all those goals against us a couple of months before the Final, I avoided him afterwards, although we knew each other well because we had met up on holidays in Majorca when George Best baby-sat our kids on the beach!

"I hated losing, full stop, but I especially hated losing to Everton because I

HOW THEY GOT THERE

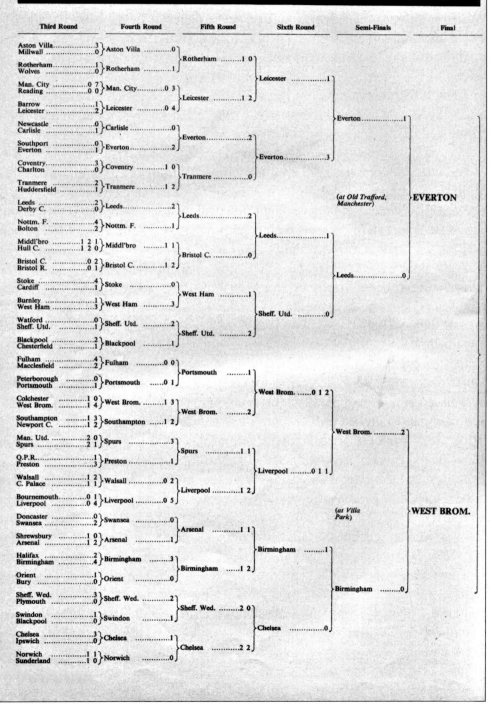

Third Round	Fourth Round	Fifth Round	Sixth Round	Semi-Finals	Final

Aston Villa..................3
Millwall ....0 } Aston Villa 0
Rotherham.................1
Wolves ....0 } Rotherham 1
Rotherham 1 0
Man. City 0 7
Reading ....0 0 } Man. City...........0 3
Leicester 1 2
Barrow 1
Leicester ....2 } Leicester 0 4
Leicester 1
Newcastle 0
Carlisle ....1 } Carlisle 0
Everton..................2
Southport 0
Everton ....1 } Everton 2
Everton 1
Coventry...................3
Charlton ....0 } Coventry 1 0
Tranmere 0
Everton 3
Tranmere 2
Huddersfield ....1 } Tranmere 1 2
Everton 1

Leeds 2
Derby C. ....0 } Leeds............2
Leeds 2
Nottm. F. 4
Bolton ....2 } Nottm. F. 1
Leeds.................1
Middl'bro 1 2 1
Hull C. ....1 2 0 } Middl'bro 1 1
Bristol C. 0
Bristol C. 0 2
Bristol R. ....0 1 } Bristol C. 1 2
Leeds..................0

Stoke 4
Cardiff ....1 } Stoke 0
West Ham 1
Burnley 1
West Ham ....3 } West Ham 3
Sheff. Utd. 0
Watford 0
Sheff. Utd. ....1 } Sheff. Utd. 2
Sheff. Utd. 2
Blackpool 2
Chesterfield ....1 } Blackpool 1

Fulham 4
Macclesfield ....2 } Fulham 0 0
Portsmouth 1
Peterborough 0
Portsmouth ....1 } Portsmouth 0 1
West Brom. 0 1 2
Colchester 1 0
West Brom. ....1 4 } West Brom. 1 3
West Brom. 2
Southampton 1 3
Newport C. ....1 2 } Southampton 1 2
West Brom. 2

Man. Utd. 2 0
Spurs ....2 1 } Spurs 3
Spurs 1 1
Q.P.R....................1
Preston ....3 } Preston 1
Liverpool 0 1 1
Walsall 1 2
C. Palace ....1 1 } Walsall 0 2
Liverpool 1 2
Bournemouth.........0 1
Liverpool ....0 4 } Liverpool 0 5

Doncaster 0
Swansea ....2 } Swansea 0
Arsenal 1 1
Shrewsbury 1 0
Arsenal ....1 2 } Arsenal 1
Birmingham 1
Halifax 2
Birmingham ....4 } Birmingham 3
Birmingham 1 2
Orient 1
Bury ....0 } Orient 0
Birmingham 0

Sheff. Wed. 3
Plymouth ....0 } Sheff. Wed. 2
Sheff. Wed. 2 0
Swindon 1
Blackpool ....0 } Swindon 1
Chelsea 0
Chelsea 3
Ipswich ....0 } Chelsea 1
Chelsea 2 2
Norwich 1 1
Sunderland ....1 0 } Norwich 0

EVERTON (at Old Trafford, Manchester)

WEST BROM. (at Villa Park)

EVERTON

147

had to go back up to an area of the country where all of their fans would be gloating at my expense. It was a nightmare and the thought of what would happen if we lost the Final was an extra incentive for me."

Cup Final day dawned happily for Alan Ashman when he was named as Westclox "Tomorrow's Top Manager" by a panel of leading journalists. The award came complete with a cheque for £500 and was decided by a clear majority after he had finished runner-up to Coventry City's Jimmy Hill the year before.

Joint 1968 runners-up were Dave Sexton (Chelsea), Alec Stock (QPR) and Malcolm Allison (no 2 to Joe Mercer at Manchester City), Ashman also being nominated for the Manager of the Year award that had gone earlier in the week to Manchester United legend Matt Busby.

Graham Williams roomed with left-winger 'Chippy' Clark and found much of the preparations as they might have been for a League game at Tottenham or Chelsea. The same could not be said of the masses back home, 16,000 of whom had tickets, backed up by a secondary contingent of several hundred who were heading for London anyway and hoping to somehow get into the stadium.

Sixty coaches left the Throstle Clubs at West Bromwich and Warley, contributing to heavy traffic on the A5 and M6 between 8am and 9.30am and mile-long queues later where the M1 joins the North Circular Road. With five special trains pulling out of New Street, the Black Country was quiet and many town centre shopkeepers saw the writing on the wall.

In the countdown to Wembley, morale and business soared, with one Smethwick confectioner seizing a market opportunity by making sponge cakes in Albion colours. Dozens of shops had similarly decorated window displays and many assistants wore blue and white rosettes and boaters - the hats also being mass-produced to capture the moment. Come Cup Final day, though, many shopkeepers closed, resigned as they were to poor trade.

Back at the team hotel, the nerves were kicking in. Young Tony Brown, then looked after in digs in Warley by a Mr and Mrs Upton, admitted he felt edgy. So did Jeff Astle, although he later said succinctly of match-day morning: "We just got up, had breakfast and a game of cards, and then got ready to go off to Wembley. It was fantastic. The atmosphere on Cup Final day is brilliant."

There was the extra distraction of the television cameras, with Cup Final Grandstand going on air at 11.15am and the commercial channel equivalent an hour and a quarter later. And Astle, whose mother Edith and stepfather Harry were on board a special family minibus to London, was happy to be put forward as the celebrity turn off the field as well as the star turn on it.

Ian Collard was one of the youngest members of the squad at 20 and says: "I was totally in awe of the Cup Final experience. Although I had been to

Wembley in the 1967 League Cup, this was completely different. I remember coming downstairs in the hotel and seeing the senior players being interviewed for TV. I did my best to keep away because I was very nervous of the occasion. I didn't think I had anything to say. I was a young, naïve kid."

Albion's players were in the safe hands of Eric Bedworth, a 38-year-old from Walsall who had also been at the wheel of their Don Everall coach en route for the League Cup Final the previous season. And, for the last few miles to the stadium, there were again two passengers on board in addition to the squad, management and directors: Journalists Ray Matts and Dennis Shaw.

Chairman Jim Gaunt had explained to the duo before lunch that it would be difficult for them to take their usual places on the coach because of the joint protocol of Wembley and the TV cameras. But Graham Williams wasn't having them fighting through the crowds on the underground and told them: "You've been with us throughout this run. You're coming with us today."

The skipper, as was his style, took the matter to higher authorities and it wasn't long before the two scribes were placing their bags on board as well. The only concession was that they would be picked up a few yards down the road at a pre-arranged spot, so the players could be filmed by TV getting on the bus without any 'infiltrators.'

"I couldn't have got any closer to an FA Cup Final without playing in one," Ray Matts added. "I was that much part of it that I felt like a substitute who didn't go on. I enjoyed covering Coventry's win over Tottenham in 1987 but I was never that interested in Finals again. They didn't mean much to me. In 1968, I was with the team I had grown up with. I was with my mates."

On the short journey to the stadium, the sight of the multi-decorated hordes, with scarves and hats more prevalent than today and with replica shirts hardly thought of, convinced the last few sceptics that this was, indeed, a very big occasion. The fans gathered on street corners, outside pubs and in front of shops and formed a backcloth that stirred the spirit yet further.

Then there were more of the media calls that were an ordeal for some - but not the camera-friendly Jeff Astle. As Albion fans spotted him in his black coat and chanted his name while he had a pre-match walk on the pitch, he was called over by Kenneth Wolstenholme for a last interview, the veteran commentator shielding them both from the steady rain with a large umbrella.

Graham Williams' previous visits to the stadium (three of them with Wales) had not been successful; four defeats out of four. But at least he had experience of the place and regarded that as priceless. "I made it my business on Final day to make sure the less experienced lads in our side were okay," he said. "We had taken a bat and ball with us to the match and used all the open space in the dressing-room to have a game of cricket.

"It was a case of doing anything to keep the mind off the match for a little bit longer. But still nothing can really prepare you for it. Standing in that tunnel waiting to be called out on the long walk to the pitch is the most nerve-racking thing in football. And, when you file out into the daylight and see 100,000 faces at the same time that the fans see you, the noise is deafening. It can frighten the life out of a young player."

Collard was one of those young players - and a long way from home. He was born in the 2,000-population former mining village of Easington in County Durham and, via some down-to-earth family advice, had been warned by his proud grandmother not to chew gum when he was introduced to Princess Alexandra!

"Before the game, the doctor asked me if I needed a tablet," he recalls. "I was tense but I was also incredibly excited and ready to go. I was standing in the tunnel and I can remember the noise the studs made on the concrete. I couldn't wait to get out there. It was a tremendous feeling. The hair on the back of your neck stood up. It was absolutely electric."

Collard had scored both goals in the League hammering at the hands of Everton two months earlier and the keeper he beat was in a worse state than he was on Cup Final afternoon. At 25, Gordon West was no spring chicken but was so badly afflicted by nerves even before run-of-the-mill games that he was often physically sick in the dressing-room. If there was one occasion guaranteed to test his stomach, it was this one.

John Talbut was calm by comparison. Having been a reserve at the stadium for an England v Scotland schoolboy international, an England v Wales full international and the 1962 Tottenham v Burnley FA Cup Final, then been cup-tied for the 1967 Albion v QPR League Cup Final, he knew the drill well and had more than deserved his chance.

"I had walked up and down that tunnel so many times, I could do it blindfolded," he said beforehand. "Now, I'm looking forward to going out on the pitch and playing!"

For his defensive partner John Kaye, the magnitude of the occasion was brought home by Wembley's ritual rendition of Abide With Me - the favourite hymn of King George V. The singing sent a cold shiver down his back, and he recalls: "When you are in the tunnel, with all the steam, being held back before you go on the pitch, it's a nervous time. But, as soon as the game starts, you are concentrating so hard that you don't notice the crowd."

Jeff Astle was in possession of a good-luck telegram from his birthplace, the Nottinghamshire town of Eastwood, while Graham Lovett's messages for the big day included one from his former school, Sheldon Heath Comprehensive. Hovering among all the players, nervous or composed, was skipper Williams, once more demonstrating what strong stuff he was made of.

When traipsing off Wembley after the League Cup Final embarrassment against QPR, he had taken a look back over his shoulder and promised himself: "We'll be back here next season - and this time in the FA Cup Final." Now, with his pledge fulfilled, he clenched his fists, looked into the eyes of his faithful team-mates and sounded the rallying call.

"Right, we're not a young side," he said. "Most of us are 28 and 29 and we might not come this way again. There may not be any more chances like this. Let's go and do it. Let's go and win that Cup!"

With those stirring words, he turned for the door. Clive Clark cleared his mouth and John Osborne, nervously bouncing a ball, said: "Don't worry, lads. They won't score today." There was just time for Alan Ashman to unwrap himself a polo, then it was off into the din and the daylight - for the biggest afternoon of their football lives.

Shall we mention the FA Cup Final now? Rival bosses Harry Catterick and Alan Ashman lead out their expectant players for the eagerly awaited 1968 Wembley showpiece.

Saturday, May 18

ALBION 1
Astle 92

EVERTON 0

ALBION	V	EVERTON
John Osborne	1	Gordon West
Doug Fraser	2	Tommy Wright
Graham Williams	3	Ray Wilson
Tony Brown	4	Howard Kendall
John Talbut	5	Brian Labone
John Kaye	6	Colin Harvey
Graham Lovett	7	Jimmy Husband
Ian Collard	8	Alan Ball
Jeff Astle	9	Joe Royle
Bobby Hope	10	John Hurst
Clive Clark	11	Johnny Morrissey
(for Kaye, FT) Dennis Clarke	12	Roger Kenyon

Attendance: 99,665
Ref: L Callaghan (Merthyr Tydfil)

Cup Winners!

Albion had chosen Goodison Park, of all places, to first show off their new all red change strip in 1966-67. The likeness to arch rivals Liverpool's colours had brought a torrent of boos from Everton supporters that day and, with a total disregard for royal protocol, Goodison diehards subjected Princess Alexandra to similar treatment when her red outfit became visible as she strode out to be introduced to the sides before kick-off!

It was the last formal act for the players before they could break, gulp in a few breaths of Wembley's highly-charged air and loosen their taut limbs in the kick-in. Almost four months of FA Cup turmoil had come down to this; a match watched by millions and carrying incalculable pride and prestige for the winners. The talking and preparations were over. Show-time!

Brian Labone spun the coin, his counterpart Graham Williams called right and, as he sometimes did, opted to kick off rather than have the more usual choice of ends. As a result, Albion found themselves attacking the tunnel end in the first half.

The opening exchanges were scrappy in the extreme. Fouls and other stoppages were plentiful and, when openings did come, they were no more than half-chances and were snatched at, Jimmy Husband missing the target as John

Graham Lovett leaves Ray Wilson in an untidy heap as his advance into Everton's area is headed off by the covering Howard Kendall.

153

Gordon West tips over under pressure from goal-poaching winger Clive Clark (left) and Graham Lovett.

Osborne lay injured after pushing out a John Morrissey cross. Then, Tony Brown hooked over as he arrived late on to Graham Lovett's centre following a header on by Jeff Astle to Williams' free-kick.

The Cup Final had an unfortunate reputation at the time for serious injuries - Manchester United keeper Ray Wood in 1957, Blackburn defender Dave Whelan in 1960 and Liverpool left-back Gerry Byrne in 1965 among them. And it wasn't long before Albion threatened to add to the list.

Doug Fraser became the first casualty when he had to be carried over the touchline for treatment to his left knee following a challenge on Morrissey. In his marker's absence, the winger burst clear into the vacant space on Albion's right but John Kaye raced across and covered superbly.

Osborne, who was himself struggling after a whack across the fingers in the opening minutes, brilliantly collected a curling cross by Tommy Wright, who, following Fraser's return after two minutes with his left knee bandaged, also needed treatment, in his case as a result of a clash of heads with Clive Clark.

Tony Brown resumed from a heavy challenge holding his back before Kaye, spoken to by referee Leo Callaghan for a meaty challenge on Alan Ball, joined the victims' list with a painful ankle. Once more, Albion's deep resolve was being tested. They had been met adversity at every stage of their Cup run and now their big day at Wembley was in danger of going the same way.

Less committed characters than Fraser and Kaye might well have departed early from the battleground. But they grimly stuck it out while Albion's bench kept a close eye on Osborne, who was now complaining about his left shoulder.

There were no goalkeeper substitutes in those days and all Alan Ashman could hope was that at least part of his popular no 1's problem was his by now famous hypochondria!

The Final everyone had expected to be a classic wasn't a pretty sight at all and the Everton fans struck up a chant of 'We Want Football' when Kaye clattered into his opposite no 6 Colin Harvey. Despite a couple of Albion corners that relieved the steady pressure at the other end, there hadn't been a serious shot or header to test either keeper in the first 35 minutes.

Finally, Morrissey let fly and Osborne did well to tip over but the first half had been dreadful; well down to the standards of the 1965 Final between Liverpool and Leeds. Jeff Astle would probably have walked out on it and sat on the team bus had he not been playing!

The second period wasn't much better, although, from an Albion attacking point of view, it was an improvement. Bobby Hope delivered a free-kick into the area after being brought down by John Hurst but, unlike at Portsmouth in the fifth round, Jeff Astle steered his well-intentioned header just the wrong side of the post. Then Ball nodded off target from Morrissey's centre when Joe Royle was better placed behind him.

But the best chances fell to Jimmy Husband, who promptly missed the lot. The Everton winger had a game to forget and was left particularly shame-faced in the dying minutes when, with his team applying mounting pressure in their pursuit of victory, he got under a free header and put it over Albion's bar.

Earlier, he had fired wide and badly mistimed another headed chance during a half in which Kaye successfully patrolled the line to clear Royle's header with Osborne out of goal. It was one of Kaye's last contributions. His injured ankle seized up after the whistle had blown at the end of 90 unattractive minutes.

Albion were fortunate to have a fellow defender on the bench and Dennis Clarke became the first substitute ever to be used in an FA Cup Final. With no sign of Everton no 12 Roger Kenyon, the underdogs at least had one set of fresh legs, although their management team claimed to have them one up on their opponents in terms of fitness.

The brief break before extra-time gave Alan Ashman and Stuart Williams the chance to get to their exhausted players and apply a little psychology. Williams, taking a quick glance over his shoulder and noticing several Everton players rolling their socks down, shouted: "Look! They're more knackered than you are! Now, pull your socks up and get back out there."

Coincidence or otherwise, the golden breakthrough came only two minutes into overtime. Fraser, switched to left-half with Clarke's arrival, carried the ball well into Everton's half and played a short pass from which Astle advanced and thumped a long-range right-foot shot against his marker Brian Labone.

Little explanation required: Albion 1 Everton 0 (Astle 92). An historic moment in time.

The ball could have cannoned anywhere but bounced back into Astle's stride and, by now on the edge of the penalty area, the striker wielded his other leg to great effect by smacking a first-time shot high and wide of Gordon West, who took no more than a short step towards his left before his net bulged. Albion were in front!

It was a double breakthrough, the sun having just poked out for the first time on a grey, rainy afternoon that had added a slippery element to turf that was famous for bringing on cramp attacks. But Astle's ninth Cup goal of the season was the occurrence that mattered - brought about by the same left foot that had found the net against Liverpool and Birmingham.

The horse racing lover, who was once known to run behind the goal during a home match to ask fans who had won the 3.30, and who famously stopped Alan Ashman doing a team-talk because he wanted to watch a race on the dressing-room TV, had put Albion in sight of the finishing line. But they still had 28 minutes to survive.

The Final had been a suffocating, subdued affair, with the flair players often shackled and the fear of losing taking over. With the lead, though, came some belated chance-making from Albion, albeit largely on the break as Everton stretched themselves looking for an equaliser.

There were relatively few alarms around John Osborne's goal either while defending the scoreboard end in the first half of extra-time or, in the last 15 minutes, the tunnel end at which Astle had gloriously struck. And it would have been 2-0 had the clearly shattered Graham Lovett not blazed wildly over the bar when a break down the right by Tony Brown teed up a clear chance.

It didn't matter unduly. Leo Callaghan's final whistle sounded just after and Albion had won the FA Cup. The team whose run had all but ended at the very place that it started, Colchester, had earned the right to climb those famous 39 steps as Wembley winners. The glory was theirs.

The combination of exhaustion and emotional outpouring consumed Alan Ashman's players. Some sunk to their knees, some hugged colleagues and some wandered round in something like a daze, perhaps trying to take in what they had achieved. Their manager, the former chicken farmer, remained outwardly calm in his moment of triumph.

No-one was more relieved at the end than John Osborne. After Albion had taken the lead, the keeper struck up a dialogue with photographers behind his goal, although the only topic of conversation centred on enquiries as to how long was left. "For about ten minutes, they kept telling me the whistle was about to go," he said. "Until we scored, I was all right, then I became as nervous as a kitten, wondering whether we could hold on. I never want to go through that again."

Osborne was a born worrier and what his widow Jenny affectionately calls 'an incredible moaner,' so the FA Cup Final was guaranteed to have him living on his nerves. "I kept goal for 107 minutes with one hand," he added. "I thought I had done something serious to my shoulder when I went down to make a save early on. But, although it was painful all through, I would never have come off and, fortunately, there weren't too many shots to deal with."

At the other end of the field was a centre-forward who had scored his first FA Cup goal four seasons earlier when playing for Notts County in a 2-1 win against little-known Frickley Colliery. Now, he had scored his 12th and done it

Proudest moment of the proudest day for Albion players and supporters.

in front of a television audience of millions and almost 100,000 spectators.

Jeff Astle had followed Sandy Brown (Tottenham), Ellis Rimmer (Sheffield Wednesday), Frank O'Donnell (Preston North End), Charlie Wayman (Preston North End), Stan Mortensen (Blackpool), Jackie Milburn (Newcastle United) and Nat Lofthouse (Bolton Wanderers) in becoming only the eighth man in history to score in every round of the FA Cup.

"I wouldn't say it was the greatest goal I had ever scored but it was the most important," he said. "It was like someone up there was saying 'Let Jeff Astle score the winning goal because he has scored in every round so far.' Somebody tried to bring me down in midfield and it could have been a free-kick but the referee played the advantage and I ran about 15 yards and tried a shot which hit someone up the backside. It came back on to my left foot and I hit it so cleanly that nobody moved and it screamed into the top of the net."

There was no great sense of imagination in the choice of tune played by the Band of the Royal Marines as the post-match formalities were about to begin; Cliff Richard's Eurovision Song Contest hit 'Congratulations' boomed out and it was music to Albion supporters' ears.

Their side had added the scalp of Everton to that of Liverpool at the end of a season in which they had done the double over League champions Manchester City and thrashed runners-up Manchester United. They had broken the dominance of Merseyside, Manchester and London, so football owed them a thank-you; if not for the Final itself, then for their victory.

Of the end-of-match feelings, midfielder Ian Collard said: "For the first five minutes after the game, I didn't know what to do. I just sat on the pitch. Then I found Tony Brown and gave him a hug, and Jeff Astle and the manager as well. We were all hugging each other.

"Then that emotion goes and, for a few seconds, I thought about the losing side and realised that could have been us. Graham Williams had a bit of a job calling us together to get our medals. I'd be a liar if I said it wasn't a very moving moment. We got together for the team photo, then we each held up the Cup to the crowd. I got the lid and wasn't giving it to anybody!

"In the dressing-room, we had our private celebrations. Some players were silent, some were jumping all over the place, popping champagne corks against the ceiling. There were different emotions for everybody and it was an awesome day; one I will never forget."

John Kaye didn't do much jumping around. His injured ankle saw to that. He even had to cut short his participation in the celebrations at pitch-side although he dragged himself behind Graham Williams up to the Royal Box to receive his medal. Among the delighted bystanders was Jesse Pennington, the captain of Albion's 1912 FA Cup Final side. He was by now 84.

"The disappointing thing was I got injured only about 20 minutes into the game," the lionhearted Kaye recalls. "I did my ankle while trying to slow Alan Ball up a bit and let him know he couldn't do just what he liked. He had always caused us problems, so we thought if we could stop him playing, Everton wouldn't be anything like as big a threat.

"I went over on my ankle, strapped it up at half-time but still couldn't turn on it. It blew up badly at full-time and Dennis Clarke went on. It was a struggle to get up to the Royal Box at the end but I managed it in my tracksuit. I couldn't do the lap of honour, though, which was disappointing. I knew it would take a long while and I was in agony. I carried the base of the Cup and went off alone to the dressing-room. It was a bad injury.

"I was upset at missing part of the celebrations but also absolutely delighted at the result. I didn't notice the atmosphere that much during the game. But, before and after, wow! No-one expected us to win and Everton were probably the better team as far as the possession was concerned. But we had a bit of luck and we defended well. I can't say they had proper chances to score."

Trainer Stuart Williams, disappointed when left out of the Baggies' 1954 Cup-winning side in favour of the more experienced Joe Kennedy, had again been busy with the magic sponge and the other contents of a kit bag that had plenty of air-time on TV!

Of the big gash in which Doug Fraser required three stitches in his knee at

Shattered limbs, happy faces.....from left: Graham Williams, Dennis Clarke, Tony Brown, Ian Collard, Graham Lovett and Clive Clark. Background: Jeff Astle, Doug Fraser.

half time, he said: "It was deep but there wasn't much blood. I bandaged him up on the touchline and he went back into the fray before we had a proper look at half-time. They were great to look after like that. How could you hope for a better bunch of players?

"Everton were a good-class side but I felt we could beat them even though they had had that big win at our place a few weeks earlier. My memory of the League game was that they had six shots and scored six goals. It was a big shock to the system but, generally, we were improving all the time, especially at the back.

"At Wembley, we had some luck in normal time as they missed chances. But, in the break before extra-time, Alan and I tried a bit of psychology and tried to convince our lads they weren't as tired as the Everton players. Jeff scored a couple of minutes later, so maybe it worked!"

Bobby Hope reckons Everton's League double over Albion in 1967-68 might have played a sub-conscious part in the Baggies' subdued performance. "Sometimes, that sticks in your mind and you show a team too much respect," he said. "You can become too wary of what your opponents are capable of.

"The defence kept us in the game for the first hour, then we started to pick it up a bit. Towards the end, we were getting on top and I fancied us to win it in extra-time. Yes, we were tired, but the goal worked wonders for us. I would not have relished chasing from a goal behind with all the weariness there was at that stage."

Kaye's injury brought recognition in the history books to Dennis Clarke, although it was only through a friend pointing out an entry in the Guinness Book of Firsts decades later that he realised he was then the only substitute ever to have gone on in an FA Cup Final! His arrival has also become the subject of a question in Trivial Pursuit and on many electronic pub games.

"I've won money myself in bars by answering the question," Clarke revealed. "But I didn't know for 20 years or more that I had been the first sub to go on in the Final. A friend had to point it out to me after he had read it. I was desperate to play in the first place and was a bit disappointed only to be named for the bench.

"Substitutes were very rarely used in those days unless there was an injury. I thought I was only there to carry the tracksuit tops off at the start. But I have to say now that it was a magnificent occasion to be part of. We never thought for a minute that we would lose and that just about summed up the team. We developed a great mental strength.

"When I played at centre-half in the League Cup Final the year before, I only knew 20 minutes beforehand that Stan Jones was unfit and I was in. I wasn't really prepared. But, against Everton, we could all see that Yorky Kaye was struggling and I went on for him at the start of extra-time. I'm sure it's only coincidence that we scored almost as soon as I stripped off.

"If I played, Doug Fraser moved forward from right-back to wing-half and it was Duggie who carried the ball forward at the start of the move from which Jeff scored. It was a magical moment and sparked all those celebrations at the end. Mind you, I was restrained. Apart from lighting up a once-a-year cigar at the banquet, I held back. I didn't have a drink all night because I wanted to savour the occasion and make sure I remembered everything."

Many of Albion's players were seen with a telling white line on their top lips when accosted for the customary television interviews after the game. But the liquid refreshment in front of the cameras was something less intoxicating than Guinness. Their tie-up with the Milk Marketing Board had guaranteed that!

Graham Williams did not try to pull the wool over anyone's eyes about the quality of the match. "It has to have been one of the worst ever Cup Finals," he admitted. "But the result is what matters and that was fantastic. Everybody said Albion v Everton would be a classic, with plenty of goals and with Everton winning. But there was hardly any football played.

"We had all felt confident we could do it and were ready for the battle. Nobody talked about losing. That was the mentality. We took that feeling out

One big shiny Cup and a couple of paper ones! From left: Stuart Williams, John Talbut, Tony Brown, Graham Williams, Clive Clark and Graham Lovett replace lost fluid.

on the pitch with us again, as we had all the way through the Cup run, and it seems irrelevant now that the quality of our performance wasn't all that it might have been."

One newspaper said three Albion players had admitted they had found themselves 'as tight as clams and fearful of error,' although they had gone to Wembley promising themselves they would play their normal game. "It was backs-to-the-wall for us," Williams added. "But we defended strongly. We had some luck yet we also had the clear chances to have won 3-0.

"Ossie took one cross near the end and threw it out to Bomber Brown, who went off on a run with an exhausted Graham Lovett in support and shouting: 'Don't pass to me! Don't pass to me!' He did and Shuv ballooned a great opportunity over the bar."

Brown recalls: "Shuv later confessed to us that he had closed his eyes, taken a real swing at it with his right foot and waited for the roar from the Albion fans. When none came and there were groans instead, he knew he had missed! Over the years, we have given him a fair bit of stick over it."

Lovett put his miss down to 'a confidence thing' but the retrieval of the ball from the running track wasted a few more seconds and there was a silver lining - for Jeff Astle. "Big Jeff said to me afterwards that he was glad I had fluffed it," the youngster added. "Otherwise, he wouldn't have been the man whose goal won the FA Cup Final. Only he could get away with saying that!"

Many years later, Lovett added: "I don't think it ever entered our heads that we might lose, although Everton were red-hot favourites. We just felt it was our year. We had that luck at Colchester with the disallowed last-minute goal and we just became stronger and stronger. There was a wonderful battling quality about the team."

Alan Ashman could have gone down in history as one of the few top-flight bosses whose side had lost at the first hurdle of both domestic knockouts to Third Division teams. Instead, he was a hero! He had followed Stuart McMillan (Derby, 1946), Stan Cullis (Wolves, 1949), Duggie Livingstone (Newcastle, 1955) and Vic Buckingham (Albion, 1954) and become only the fifth manager in 23 post-war seasons to lift the FA Cup in their first full year in a job.

He retained a slightly blinkered, even tongue-in-cheek view of a Final that was a disappointment for all except Albion diehards. "It was a super game as far as I'm concerned," he recalled. "It was a cracker and we won it. What more do you want?

"Everton had beaten us 6-2 at The Hawthorns and Alan Ball scored four. He was one of the really great players and always seemed to score against us. But he never looked like scoring at Wembley and that says it all. John Kaye took care of him early on. He tackled him and the message got through quickly.

"I suppose, after 90 minutes, I felt a little disappointed at how things were going. I remember I kept shouting out instructions and muttering to myself - a sure sign that I was not satisfied. But the players have shown over the season that they are a very adaptable side and are difficult to beat.

"I don't think either ourselves or Everton set out to play defensively. There was a lot of close marking and hard tackling, and that dictated the flow of the game rather than any cautious attitude. But it wasn't a dirty game."

Victory meant Albion would be competing in the 1968-69 European Cup Winners' Cup, two seasons after they had made their debut in Continental competition by playing in the Inter Cities Fares Cup. It was an attractive proposition and Ashman was already looking forward to pitting his wits against managers from overseas.

"I'm not frightened of Europe, although it's obviously going to be something different," he said. "Our achievements have shown we have the players and the method. Any team who can come out on top after seven hours of Cup football against Liverpool and Everton must have something more than promise. With a better start in the First Division, we could even have been thinking of the League and Cup double."

Ashman, a proud man and, at 39, one of the brightest managerial talents in

Arise the Cup winners! From left: Clive Clark, John Osborne, Doug Fraser and Graham Williams stand to take the applause from both their womenfolk and the other guests at the Cup Final night banquet at London's Park Lane Hotel.

football, appreciated his players going through the pain barrier in the cause. He wondered whether Doug Fraser would be able to go out for the second half but said: "He just shrugged his shoulders and got himself ready to go out again. He's that sort of man. When players like he and John Kaye register agony on their faces, you know they are hurt. They showed terrific guts in carrying on."

John Osborne and John Talbut each chose Cup Final day to have one of their best games for the club. Osborne was not that troubled by shots and headers at his goal but his immaculate handling filled his defenders with confidence and kept Everton's dangerous forwards at arm's length. His pre-match promise of 'No goals at my end today' had been carried out.

Talbut was every bit as commanding and seemed to have a magnet embedded in his forehead, such was his aerial command in and around Albion's penalty area. "All the way through the Cup run, I thought we would do it," he said. "Once we had that escape at Colchester, I was convinced we were going all the way. We were a bit down after we had only drawn at home to Liverpool but we seemed to get stronger after that.

"Among my guests at the Final was an on old schoolmate of mine from the north-east who had briefly been with Sunderland and whose father was a bookmaker. We were chatting after the game and I casually asked what odds I might get for another Albion v Everton Final in 1969. I'm not a betting man but the odds were very long and I took the bet."

Bill Shankly is once reputed to have gone round his dressing-room after a game to check his side's discarded shirts. He would hold up what he decided was the heaviest one and say it belonged to the player who had sweat the most in the cause. Had Alan Ashman been similarly inclined, he would have needed help in lifting some of the white jerseys that Saturday teatime.

"At the final whistle, we were shattered," said skipper Graham Williams. "All the celebration photographs on the pitch show the looks of exhaustion. Everyone could see we had put so much into the game. Everton went up for their medals first and weren't happy. Alan Ball didn't speak to me. He went straight off and apparently gave his medal away.

"When we got back to the hotel, nobody wanted to go out for a drink. We were all too tired to celebrate. We had the banquet at the Park Lane Hotel, where Bob Monkhouse was the comedian. Jim Gaunt stood up and said he was growing a bit tired of all these Wembley Cup Finals. What he really wanted was the League title. He was a gruff man, always smoking cigars, and apparently not over-impressed with the lovely shiny FA Cup standing in front of him.

"It was water off a duck's back to the players because we knew what Jim was like. But I remember the wives were a bit put out. They didn't think much of his comments because they loved a good day out at Wembley. For one thing, they knew it meant they would be able to go out and buy a new outfit!

"After the banquet, we went to the Sportsman's Club which we couldn't get into, although Everton's players were already in. The doormen seemed to think there might be some trouble. When we finally went to bed, a lot of us couldn't sleep. The adrenalin was incredible. We even tried baths to unwind, and a crowd of us got up at some ridiculously early hour and sat in the foyer chatting before heading off to Petticoat Lane market."

Jeff Astle, whose winning goal was shown again during a 50-minute Match of the Day highlights programme late at night, was one of those overtaken by insomnia and said: "I never went to bed that night. We sat up with Kenneth Wolstenholme and his wife, then we went for a walk in the park when it was light and couldn't wait to get our hands on the newspapers."

Photographs, including one that has found its way into this publication, subsequently proved that Astle did more than sit and chat. He found a stage, he had his audience and was delighted to use the FA Cup as a prop as he treated his team-mates to a musical interlude.

Alan Ashman was another to receive a lot of back-slapping. He may have given the impression of being laid-back but, when congratulated by the Press the following day for being so cool through the endless media interviews, he

Jeff Astle, the life and soul of every party, didn't really need to beat the drums for Albion and himself. His 35 goals for the season, nine of them in the FA Cup, did that. Picture courtesy of Associated Newspapers.

replied: "You should have seen me in my hotel room afterwards. I was beating the wall with my fists shouting 'Yes!'"

In actual playing time, Albion's Cup triumph had lasted an incredible 16 hours - six lots of 90 minutes, three replays, one second replay and two slabs of stamina-sapping extra-time. If knockout football is a sprint and the League a marathon, then this was at least a middle-distance race. With stoppage-time added on here and there, they had played the equivalent of more than a quarter of a First Division programme in lifting the Cup.

In playing minutes, they had required almost twice as long as their 1954 counterparts to emerge triumphant, making this by far their longest run in the competition and probably their furthest-reaching, given that they had called en route at Colchester, Southampton, Portsmouth, Liverpool, Manchester, Birmingham, London and, in four of the build-ups, at Southport.

Well before the age of football superstars and massively-paid, over-hyped individuals, they had struck a blow for the rank and file. They were a bunch of down-to-earth blokes, who preferred a game of dominoes to courting publicity in the tabloids. They had combined their talent with sheer hard work to bring Albion one of the best days in their history.

Living Like Kings

The first full day of Albion's reign as FA Cup holders dawned on a shock note. An article in the Sunday People claimed Bobby Hope wanted a transfer. Homesickness gnawed away at the brilliant midfielder throughout a playing career of more than 20 years and he never completely staved off the burning desire to play for his beloved Glasgow Rangers.

Hope had always been in demand, no fewer than 20 senior clubs chasing him when he was a pupil at Clydebank High School and, after playing in Albion's Central League side at 15 and the first team a year later, the talent-spotters were still on his trail.

Only Willie Penman's refusal to move from Ibrox to Albion - the Rangers reserve inside-forward later joined Newcastle - had prevented Hope going north earlier while talks between the midfielder and Arsenal were later lined up for the unusual setting of Knutsford Service Station on the M6 until Alan Ashman changed his mind and said no.

The manager was disturbed to see stories about Hope gain new momentum, though, in the aftermath of the club's best day in almost a decade and a half. He

Letting the train take the strain.....Tony Brown and his fiance Irene (later his wife) share a carriage with Laraine and Jeff Astle on the journey home from London; first-class, of course. Picture courtesy of Associated Newspapers.

did all he could to reassure fans and said: "Bobby has not made a written transfer request, although we talked at the start of the season and he expressed a wish to go back to Scotland. It's my sincere hope that he stays with Albion and will be playing here next season as a full Scottish international. I'm quite sure he has enjoyed his football with us.

"He certainly hasn't been playing as though he has been unsettled and, as far as I'm concerned, there's no question of him being allowed to leave. Where would you go to replace a player like him? You can't let talent like that go and hope to build a side."

Hope was subsequently questioned by reporters and told them: "I can't settle down but I have not made a transfer request since the start of the season. I appreciate that the club have a year's option on me when my contract expires this summer and, if they won't let me go, there's nothing I can do about it. But, whatever I was offered wouldn't make any difference. It's not about money. I want to return to Scotland."

Rangers are thought to have offered £175,000 for Hope in 1968 - a figure that would have made him the costliest player in Britain at the time by some way - but Albion dug their heels in and declined it. For a club who later came to be seen as a selling one, with the likes of Laurie Cunningham, Bryan Robson and Remi Moses moving on to grander stages, it was a strong statement.

"My wife was from Wednesbury and the transfer talk was no reflection of the good things that were happening at The Hawthorns," the player now adds. "But I knew Rangers were very keen to get me. There were no agents in those

Home in triumph - skipper Graham Williams and manager Alan Ashman walk through well-wishers on the platform after their arrival back in Birmingham.

West Bromwich rejoices..... a second successive day to remember for Albion players among their supporters.

days but there were still approaches, either via a phone call from someone you didn't know or even a player.

"I had been down in England for a few years and sentiment came into it. I had always wanted to play for Rangers. They were my boyhood heroes. But the rules then were heavily weighted in the favour of the clubs. Even when your contract had expired, you still couldn't move on without their approval as they held your registration."

More than 100 miles north of where Hope and his Albion team-mates had been celebrating their FA Cup Final victory, almost 500 police were drafted in for the squad's victorious homecoming, plus a further dozen from the city of Birmingham on horseback. Needless to say, they were still hugely outnumbered by supporters.

Around 2,000 fans were at New Street to welcome Albion in and out of the railway station and the route from the city towards the Black Country via the Priory Ringway, Colmore Circus and St Chad's Circus, was heavily populated. With another 10,000 congregated outside West Bromwich Town Hall, estimates of the total turn-out ranged from 150,000 to 250,000.

The announcement of the team coach's route came with news that West Bromwich High Street would be closed from its junction with Sandwell Road to just past Dartmouth Square. All crossing roads were also out of use and bus services which operated along those routes were diverted.

Fans seemed to be in competition to find the most unusual and even most

Manager Alan Ashman, quiet and reserved by nature, takes his turn to enjoy the acclaim of the masses as he shows off the FA Cup one more time outside West Brom town hall.

dangerous look-outs. They were perched in swaying trees, on buildings (especially the post office and banks), bus shelters, up flagpoles, on window ledges and on 40ft high chimneys. Supporters in trees acted as cheerleaders and the masses joined in the singing.

The jubilant crowds were held back by police officers linking arms and were kept informed by loudspeaker of where the coach was. The same public address system played 'Congratulations' when the players were in earshot but, with individuals frequently breaking through the police cordon, the team were more than 40 minutes late reaching their final destination.

There, they entered the Lodge Road entrance of the Town Hall and were officially welcomed by the Mayor, Alderman C O Ellis, on a platform above the High Street. Skipper Graham Williams, with the Cup, led his men out on to the dias and the players took it in turns to lift the trophy, Jeff Astle and John Kaye being acknowledged the loudest.

Williams and chairman Jim Gaunt each said a few words, then the members of the Albion party went inside for cocktails and to indulge in some polite small talk with civic leaders.

Amid the euphoria down below, there was criticism from the authorities for parents who ignored warnings and allowed their youngsters to put themselves in danger at the mercy of the multitudes. Some were passed from the deepest parts of the crowd to safety over the heads of adults but 130, mainly women and juniors, were treated for crush injuries and fainting. A dozen were taken to hospital, most with suspected fractures.

Laying on special buses to get the fans home was another major task, by which time the exhausted, short-of-sleep and emotionally drained players were more than ready to step out of the limelight for a day or so. But the turn-out had left its imprint on them.

The hobbling John Kaye described the homecoming as 'fantastic' and was not alone in marvelling at some of the precarious vantage points taken up by celebrating fans. "Coming back was fantastic," he said. "I have never known anything like it. How the fans managed to find such unusual places, I will never know."

And Alan Everiss, the veteran secretary who, with his manager-secretary father Fred, achieved an unbelievable continuous family representation at the club of nearly 100 years, added: "What a wonderful reception the supporters gave us! It was a most moving day for all of us and one we will never forget."

Albion's team had been due to return to London almost immediately to appear on the Eamonn Andrews Show but had to cancel the appointment at the TV studios in the end because proceedings in the Black Country dragged on longer than expected. It was one commitment too many at a time when everybody wanted to salute them; West Bromwich Albion, the FA Cup winners.

On Merseyside, meanwhile, informed sources had talked in advance of a 200,000-strong turn-out lining an 11-mile procession route in the event of an Everton victory. In defeat, a mere fraction of that number showed up. Centre stage was left to Albion but their players didn't have long to wallow in the back-slapping.

Just two days after the joyous homecoming, they were to fly out on tour to East Africa as the follow-up to their mid-1960s tours to South America and North America. It meant yet another separation, this time considerably longer, from loved ones. But there were some wonderful memories from the weekend with which the home fires were kept burning.

"Going to Wembley was a fantastic experience for the wives as well," recalls John Osborne's widow Jenny. "We were just a group of working-class girls, married to footballers and many of us with children. We became a really close group and had a great time of our own when Albion were doing so well.

"Coming from a little village in Derbyshire, where I had gone out with John since I was 15, I couldn't believe all these trips to cup finals and then the super dinners that followed them in swish hotels. It was a taste of the high life and I remember we all got on so well.

"If anything, the banquets we had after the League Cup Finals in 1967 and 1970 were better than the one after the FA Cup Final because the players were so shattered after beating Everton and everyone seemed drained by it all. But going home to show the Cup off next day was a once-in-a-lifetime experience.

"I think the wives were downstairs on the coach with the players sitting in the open top and the crowds were tremendous. Then, when John and I got back home to Great Barr, we found that our friends and neighbours had done the house up in blue and white trimmings, with cut-outs in the shape of the FA Cup."

Jeff Astle had the same treatment, with his and wife Laraine's house in Springfield Crescent, West Bromwich, adorned by messages such as 'Well done, Jeff,' 'Astle, King of the Crescent' and 'From a Villa fan to an Albion man, well done Jeff!' The local Press photographers had a field day, one of them capturing Clive Clark's startled look as he arrived at the property.

Astle lapped up the celebrity status and, as if life wasn't hectic enough, found time to fit in a visit to see and hold two-day-old Jeffrey Astle Davis, born to proud parents John and Mary, of Hockley. Like the game, Mary had to go into extra-time, the 7lb 4oz baby arriving a week later than expected and taking in his first sight of the outside world within seconds of the winning goal flying in at Wembley.

"It was unbelievable," said Dad John. "I was watching the Final on TV and, just as Jeff's shot went in, I heard a cry. A great goal and a great baby!" There were no prizes for guessing the man whose name topped the guest list later in the summer for the christening.

The ever-amenable Astle was later to say the six-game African adventure knocked some off the shine off the FA Cup triumph; it was good celebration time lost! He might have cast an envious glance towards transfer-listed winger Kenny Stephens, who successfully sought permission to stay at home in case any enquiries came in for him.

Ray Wilson stepped aboard in his place and, on the day that Albion signed three youngsters from Scotland, including Alistair Robertson, manager Alan Ashman announced that little-known reserves Alan Merrick, Ron Potter and Pete 'Percy' Freeman were in the party to set off on tour the next day, as were Nicky Krzywicki, Ronnie Rees and Asa Hartford.

In his finest hour, Alan Ashman demonstrated that he hadn't forgotten his

Albion players still have a spring in their step as they set foot on African soil for the first time. First down the stairs are John Talbut, Graham Williams, Nick Krzywicki, John Kaye and Stuart Williams.

previous club Carlisle. They were now being managed by Tim Ward and, as Albion's jet was leaving the tarmac at Heathrow, it was disclosed that his side of FA Cup winners would be playing a pre-season friendly at Brunton Park a couple of months later.

Two notable absentees on the tour were Bobby Hope and Doug Fraser. They were not with their club colleagues because they were to fly out instead to make their full Scottish international debuts in the friendly in Holland just over a week later.

Both had played extensively along with Eddie Colquhoun on an unofficial 1967 tour by their country to Israel, Hong Kong, New Zealand, Australia and Canada when a bad injury to Ian Ure left Fraser captaining a squad containing Willie Johnston, Willie Henderson and a certain young Alex Ferguson!

In the event, Hope's proud night in Amsterdam, which had curiously began with him having 'Glasgow Rangers' listed as his club after his name in the

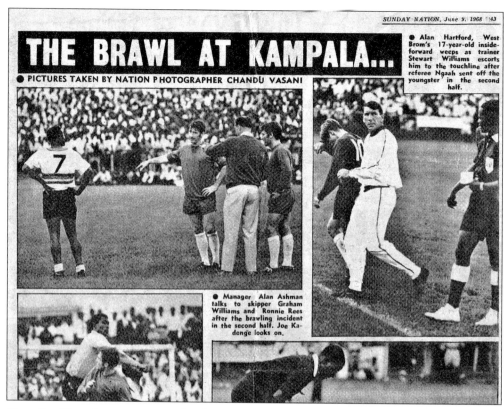

THE BRAWL AT KAMPALA...

● PICTURES TAKEN BY NATION PHOTOGRAPHER CHANDU VASANI

● Alan Hartford, West Brom's 17-year-old inside-forward weeps as trainer Stewart Williams escorts him to the touchline after referee Ngaah sent off the youngster in the second half.

● Manager Alan Ashman talks to skipper Graham Williams and Ronnie Rees after the brawling incident in the second half. Joe Kadenge looks on.

How the Ugandan newspaper the Sunday Nation portrayed Albion's 2-2 draw with an East African X1 in the capital of Kampala. Top left: Manager Alan Ashman goes on the pitch to speak to Ronnie Rees and Graham Williams. Top right: Stuart Williams escorts the sent-off Asa Hartford to the touchline. This was the fifth game of a six-match tour that ended with a 4-3 victory over the Kenya national side in Nairobi three days later.

The friendlier side of the tour, as demonstrated by (from left) John Osborne, Ray Wilson, Graham Lovett and John Talbut.

official programme, was sadly cut short. He lined up in midfield alongside his boyhood hero John Greig but suffered a foot injury that forced him off after only 19 minutes.

He had to abort plans to join the African tour - a fate that also befell Fraser, who went down for several days with a stomach disorder after facing the Dutch. Both were disappointed. There were some keen travellers in Albion's squad and Hope and Fraser would love to have taken part in another memorable trip that only football could have given them.

They had to rely on sketchy Press reports for details of Albion's progress on a tour on which it wasn't only Africa's famous game that was wild. The games were wild as well! Team-mates subsequently filled the duo in on what they had missed, one of the main talking-points being Asa Hartford's reaction to some dreadful provocation.

"I swear Asa was sent off twice in one game," Tony Brown recalls. "He had his marching orders but then went back on to the pitch to get involved all over again when trouble broke out. The referee eventually got the game restarted and young Asa stayed on the pitch for a few minutes until the officials realised what had happened and ordered him off again."

Graham Williams, who continued to travel the world with his various coaching and management postings after his playing days ended, enjoyed the trip as much as anyone and said: "It was brilliant, although the matches were tough and, in one or two cases, violent. The Africans seemed to regard playing the FA Cup winners as though they were up against the full English national team. They were really desperate to beat us.

"But it was like a holiday as well at times

Continuing the Cup-showing tour for the Albion 'family.'

and the wives went off themselves for a break. The reluctance in some quarters to go may have been because we were so exhausted after the end of the season. It really was a punishing schedule and we were shattered. But, when we got back, we had a couple of cricket days at local clubs and each player borrowed the FA Cup to take it round his home town. There was also the tour of all the Throstle Clubs to undertake to show off the trophy. That was a lovely task.

"We didn't have the Cup with us in Africa because it wasn't allowed to leave the country but we used to take it everywhere we could. I brought it home and had the pleasure of showing it off to the Everton fans! I also took it to Rhyl once and, on more than one occasion, we would have our heart in our mouth because it would go missing for a few minutes in a crowded pub before someone would bring it back after taking it outside to photograph it!"

Not everyone treated the cherished silverware with due reverence. Heather and Graham Williams' 18-month-old son Richard mistook it for a potty, sat on it and did what comes naturally to toddlers. If the Cup itself could be tarnished, though, the memories couldn't.

"It was a lovely time, although the success certainly didn't make any of us rich," Williams added. "The bonus for winning the FA Cup amounted to less than three figures each and I remember when we had reached the League Cup Final against QPR the previous season, I received an extra £25! There were no mega-stars then. Yes, there were stars of the pitch - some terrific players. But nobody in the game was earning that much more than anybody else."

While the players were on their exotic travels, the well-done congratulations poured into The Hawthorns. One came from the crew of the aircraft carrier Albion and there were others from a Birmingham City fan in Toronto, the Lima Cricket Club in Peru, which Jimmy Hagan's side had visited on their tour of South America a couple of years earlier, and the American football club Atlanta Chiefs.

The Black Country-based fans were still in celebratory mood, two of them having emerged into the night air under the influence of appropriate intake and daubed Astle Is The King in paint on the brickwork of a structure in Netherton now known as Astle's Bridge.

When it was scrubbed off by the local authority in 1993, it was rewritten within hours as: 'Astle Is The King. Please note, Dudley Council.' And official Alida Tricker said after the 'reappearance' of the words: "Perhaps the slogan is like the White Horse and part of the natural landscape."

Around 1,400 fans attended two special FA Cup Final screenings at West Bromwich's Adelphi Ballroom and further two-hour showings were planned for the following week at Warley, Stone Cross, Hateley Heath, Smethwick and the

Adelphi again. A copy was also flown out to Africa for the enjoyment of the men who had made it all possible.

A projector was laid on for the evening and the players sat down to watch the game in its entirety at their hotel. "I think it was while we were in Dar es Salaam in Tanzania," recalls Tony Brown. "I wasn't a great traveller and would have been happier back home than on tour. But it was wonderful to see the Final on screen, even if we had to admit it didn't look a great game.

"One of the directors was enjoying taking the mickey out of Graham Lovett by tutting if he misplaced a pass and saying 'There's that Lovett again.' You can imagine the banter when Shuv blasted that great chance over the bar in the last few seconds!"

By then, Alan Ashman's men knew they would kick off the 1968-69 First Division season at home to Sheffield Wednesday and Manchester United, the latter of whom became the first club team after Albion to win at the twin towers when they lifted the European Cup against Benfica on May 29.

Four days after the FA Cup Final, Everton centre-half Brian Labone returned to Wembley and this time finished on the winning side as England beat Sweden 3-1 in a friendly. He subsequently shelved the plans he had to hang up his boots and go into business.

There was one other strange spin-off to Wembley glory. Defender Dennis Clarke had arranged his wedding for Saturday, August 3, 1968, and had some buttering-up to do with Alan Ashman. As FA Cup winners, that was the day Albion would now be facing League champions Manchester City at Maine Road in the Charity Shield.

What Happened Next

Trying to follow up Wembley glory was always going to be a tall order. But, after crashing to an ill-fated 6-1 defeat at League champions Manchester City in the Charity Shield - a game in which Graham Williams was less successful than at Southampton in the role of stand-in keeper - Albion had a good dart at it in 1968-69.

They had another impressive campaign, albeit one that promised a lot and delivered little, and did so after a further addition to their long line of shocks at the hands of minnows. This time it was Fourth Division Peterborough who upset them, 2-1 in the League Cup third round. At least it was a change from being beaten by Third Division clubs!

Undeterred, Alan Ashman's side did well both in Europe and in their efforts to follow Newcastle and Tottenham as only the third club since the Second World War to lift the FA Cup in successive seasons. They overturned a first-leg 3-1 defeat to go through on away goals in an ugly European Cup Winners Cup first-round tie against Bruges, then progressed in considerable comfort against Dinamo Bucharest.

Winger Ronnie Rees, the club's record signing, was sent off in the first-leg draw in Rumania and was to move on to Nottingham Forest within months as his team-mates prospered without him. By the time Albion drew 0-0 in the first leg of the quarter-final against Dunfermline, they had kicked off their big Cup defence by winning 3-0 at home to Second Division Norwich.

John Osborne and Doug Fraser are powerless to prevent one of Manchester City's six Charity Shield goals on the day Albion returned to Maine Road, scene of their epic FA Cup victory over Liverpool less than four months earlier.

Then they won 2-1 at Fulham in round four and 1-0 at home to Arsenal in the fifth round and, although Dunfermline triumphed at The Hawthorns on such a cold night that Graham Lovett was the only one of the 22 players not to take to the pitch wearing gloves, their hold on the FA Cup remained a powerful one.

En route for a satisfactory League finish of tenth, they hit back from a goal down to win 2-1 at Chelsea in the sixth round and seemed set for Wembley again with only Leicester blocking their path. Everton, of all clubs, were up against Manchester City in the other half of the last-four draw.

But the East Midlanders, who suffered relegation to the Second Division a few weeks later, recorded a surprise 1-0 win at Hillsborough with a mis-hit late volley from Albion-supporting striker Allan Clarke. It was the club's first defeat in 14 ties in the competition stretching back nearly two and a quarter seasons and meant there was to be no FA Cup glory after all in 1969.

Graham Lovett made only seven League appearances before Christmas in 1968-69 but at least he was plagued only by football injuries. And he came strong in the second half of the season as he played another 16 First Division outings as well as starting all of the FA Cup ties and figuring in five of the six European games.

Then, unbelievably, massive misfortune struck him for the second time. The day after returning from Albion's 1969 summer tour to Canada and USA, where he had scored twice in the 12-0 slaughter of Edmonton All Stars in the final game, he was with his mother in his Rover 2000 on the way home from Halesowen.

A double-decker bus went out of control, hit their stationary car head-on, left

John Kaye, Doug Fraser and Ray Wilson provide a solid line of cover for John Osborne in the 1968-69 FA Cup semi-final against Leicester. Picture courtesy of Leicester Mercury.

him trapped for five hours and necessitated a hospital check for his mum. Thankfully, the Rover's roof stood up to the impact but Lovett's body wasn't as lucky. He suffered a broken thigh, collapsed right lung and broken right arm; another long spell on the sidelines beckoned and an aluminium pin was inserted in his thigh to hold it together. It's still there.

Back in the mid-1960s, when Lovett was earning only £12 a week at The Hawthorns, £1.50 of that went on bus fares to and from training and matches. With the benefit of hindsight, it might have been better if he had stuck to that form of transport and so avoided the two horrific car crashes in what were still his formative football years.

He wasn't seen at first-team level at all in 1969-70 until going on as a substitute in the 2-2 home draw with Newcastle on March 14. He was in the starting line-up at Burnley and at home to Tottenham in the next two matches but that was his lot for the season except for a four-game fling in the Anglo Italian Cup. He had lost another seven and a half months.

He soldiered on and played a further 21 League matches in 1970-71 but a player supposedly in his prime was now a shade slower and less mobile. He was fighting a losing battle. The £14,000 he was awarded against West Midlands Passenger Transport Executive in 1973 as a result of his second crash did not adequately compensate for his career going downhill.

The end came soon after he had a three-game loan spell at Southampton in 1972. By then, the Saints had Stuart Williams back on their books as assistant manager to Lawrie McMenemy and it's ironic that one of that trio of matches was an 8-0 defeat at Everton. As Lovett looks back now on a career sabotaged by bad luck, he can at least reflect that he was on the winning side against the Merseysiders when it really mattered.

Albion did make it back to Wembley in 1970, this time in the League Cup. They had overcome Alan Ashman's former club Carlisle in the semi-final despite losing the first leg at Brunton Park but an early goal by Jeff Astle - this one shortly after kick-off rather than at the start of extra-time - was not enough to prevent Manchester City winning 2-1.

The all white change strip was worn both in that game and in the 1969 FA Cup semi-final at Hillsborough and wasn't such a lucky kit anymore. Like the habit of going to Southport before big cup games, it was phased out and the club started to wear yellow and blue second colours. Oh, and Dennis Clarke and Ian Collard never did splash out on their TR6 and TR7!

Nor did Jim Gaunt stand down, as planned, as chairman in 1969. He still had visions of League glory and, in a hard-back 1970 publication on the club, stated in more sensitive terms, what he had preached on FA Cup Final night.

"After three Wembley appearances in four years, we're anxious to continue our flair for success in cup football," he said. "Allied to this, however, much endeavour must be made to find consistency in the League for, in the long run, it's regular weekly success that builds up a good side. It isn't beyond us, with a set-up patiently built up by Alan Ashman and his staff, to win the League title."

Gaunt didn't prove himself so patient. When Ashman was on holiday in Rhodes in 1971, the chairman who had praised his gentlemanly ways when he appointed him, didn't wait for him to set foot back on English soil. He fired him there and then, Ashman disgracefully learning of his fate from a waiter.

Ashman had presided over 201 games - exactly the same as Jimmy Hagan. His side had finished 17th and gone 16 months without an away League victory until famously winning at title-chasing Leeds in April. "Until we lift the First Division crown, we can't truly claim to have arrived," Gaunt said.

Colchester's name cropped up on Albion's fixture list again in August, 1971, and this time they beat them. The Baggies side by now managed by Don Howe and containing only four FA Cup Final survivors, drew 4-4 at home to the Essex club in the final of the Watney Cup pre-season tournament, and lost in a penalty shoot-out staged at the Smethwick End.

Revolution was coming quickly under former Albion and England full-back Howe - and not for the better. Relegation was followed by the departure of the injury-plagued Jeff Astle in 1974 and Tony Brown and John Osborne were the only remaining members of the Wembley 68 team. They stayed well beyond helping restore the club's top-flight status in 1976 but time waits for no man.

The duo also moved on eventually, the last playing link with the victory over Everton severed when Brown said his farewells at The Hawthorns in 1981 and moved on to Torquay and then Stafford Rangers at a time when he also spent two summers in American football. It was 13 years on from Wembley glory.

The club's all-time record appearance-maker and (wartime excepted) record scorer still lives in Walsall and is an ever-present watcher of Albion games for one of Birmingham's independent radio stations. Bobby Hope is chief scout at The Hawthorns and Graham Williams remains a regular visitor to the ground on PR duties and as a scout for his ex-Albion team-mate Sir Bobby Robson.

Not that Williams has to stray too far from his home in North Shropshire to be reminded of the impact of FA Cup Final success. He lives much closer to Merseyside than the Black Country and has remained very much part of the football fraternity in the subsequent 35 years.

He smiles: "The neighbours up here still say to me: 'You're the bloke who nicked the FA Cup off us.' At one point, I had not been to Goodison Park for about 20 years and was walking outside the ground when a supporter shouted: 'You pinched our Cup!' Others were less polite and said only partly under their breath: 'Lucky bastards!'"

As Time Rolled By....

John Osborne proceeded to total exactly 250 League appearances for Albion and added a further 62 outings in cup football, although he had spells in the shadows of both Jim Cumbes and Peter Latchford while also having to see off the challenge of Graham Smith. The ever-popular keeper injured his finger trying to stop Manchester City's fourth goal in the 6-1 Charity Shield slaughter at Maine Road the August after Wembley and subsequently had a plastic joint inserted - surgery that led to him being dubbed the Bionic Keeper. He also reckoned the extra body part added at least five years to his career. Remarkably for a man who seemed blighted by injury, he was still playing senior football for the club at the age of 36, more than nine years after the 1968 FA Cup Final, although he retired at one point and also went out on loan to neighbours Walsall. Played (and erred!) in the 1969 FA Cup semi-final against Leicester and lined up in the 1970 League Cup Final against Manchester City before becoming a heroic ever-present in the 1975-76 promotion campaign and keeping a club record 22 clean sheets. Made £32,000 - then a record for a Midlands player - from his testimonial in 1978 and wound down his playing career with Shamrock Rovers, Preston and Telford.

Doug Fraser's tally of more than 60 cup appearances in his eight years at The Hawthorns showed what a renowned side Albion were in knock-out football. In total, he played 325 games for the club, graduating to skipper for the losing League Cup Final against Manchester City in 1970, then he appeared in 85 League matches for Nottingham Forest after joining them in 1971. A further 27 followed for Walsall, where he was taken as a player by then manager Ronnie Allen. With the departure of the Albion legend, he stepped up to player-boss and was in charge from 1973 to 1977 in a stint that included FA Cup giant-killings of Manchester United and Newcastle and an odd-goal exit at Birmingham in the sixth round. It was at Fellows Park that the twice-capped Scottish international was sent off for striking former Hawthorns team-mate Kenny Stephens in a match at home to Bristol Rovers. "Kenny said something and my fist slipped!" he recalls. Unemployed for six months after leaving the Saddlers, Fraser bumped into Bob McKinlay while out shopping one day - and was persuaded to follow the former Nottingham Forest centre-half into the prison service. In his 22 years as a warder, he declined the chance to manage the football team at Nottingham Jail but met two renowned inmates in gangster Reggie Kray and police killer Harry Roberts.

Graham Williams had just turned 30 when he led his team-mates up the famous steps to Wembley's Royal Box in 1968 and knew the clock was ticking down on his top-flight career. His time as a Welsh international was nearly over as well but there was still a 26th and final cap to come with his country - in midfield on an unusual night in Cardiff when he found himself up against Luigi Riva in an Italy side who went on to reach the World Cup final in Mexico in 1970. The tough left-back, who had been sent off on Albion's stormy trip to Africa just after the victory over Everton, found himself seriously rivalled by Ray Wilson for the following campaign and lost out to the Scot in the race for a place in the League Cup Final defeat against Manchester City in 1970, although he had played in the away first leg of the semi-final against Carlisle and in three of the games in the earlier rounds of the competition. The last of his 314 League appearances for the club came at Derby in the middle of the following season, after which he hung his boots up and served as assistant manager at The Hawthorns before embarking on a virtual world tour in a coaching career that took him to Weymouth, Kuwait (where he linked up again with Ian Collard), Greece, Nigeria, Finland, the United Arab Emerates, Dubai and Wales, the latter as assistant manager to Bobby Gould.

Tony Brown was a mere 22-year-old on the day the FA Cup was won but proceeded to rewrite the Hawthorns' history books. His tally of 574 League appearances for the club is an Albion record, the last of his top-flight starts coming on January 1, 1980, at Ipswich - the ground where he had made his debut for the club 17 years earlier. His 279 competitive goals for the Baggies are another record (WG Richardson's wartime scoring exploits excepted) and his goal-scoring appearance in the 1978 FA Cup semi-final defeat against Ipswich was one of an astonishing 146 outings in knockout football that included three League Cup Finals. Brown became unsettled during the Don Howe reign but, revitalised under Johnny Giles, fired the club back to top-flight football with his spectacular winner in his hometown of Oldham in 1976. After 20 years at The Hawthorns, Brown had short spells at Torquay, Stafford Rangers, New England Teamen and Jacksonville Teamen before he tried his hand as a coach, first with Johnny Giles at Albion from 1984 to 1986 and then with Garry Pendrey at Birmingham from 1987 to 1989.

John Talbut had a good run for the money he invested just after the 1968 FA Cup Final. He placed a bet on Albion meeting Everton again in the following season's final and the two clubs were favourites to win their respective semi-finals in the competition, only for both to lose to late goals - by Leicester and Manchester City respectively. The centre-half played 124 consecutive games for Albion from the spring of 1967 to the autumn of 1969 but moved on at the end of 1970-71 following an appearance tally for the club of 193 that brought him a solitary one goal. Ironically, he contributed to his own departure by being sent by Alan Ashman on scouting missions and recommending the signing of an emerging Peterborough centre-half called John Wile, whom he watched in action at London Road. Talbut's own career took him into Belgian football, where he played (until 1976), managed and coached. For ten years, he also kept the FA Cup Final spirit very much alive by running a pub called Wembley 68 in the town of Mechelen, where he was instrumental in inviting Albion for a pre-season friendly in 1974-75.

John Kaye's ankle injury was so bad that he played only the last game of the Africa tour. He was restricted largely to the role of social secretary but enjoyed the trip despite what he called the 'roughhouse' football. And he never forgot his working class roots. Throughout his playing career, the one-time welder even retained his membership of the Boilermakers Union and went back into industry following a football career that took him from Albion to Hull (as player, then coach and manager) and on for a second stint with Scunthorpe (as assistant manager). Kaye's emergency switch to the role of defensive wing-half became permanent and he scored only two more League and cup goals for the

club after the FA Cup Final triumph. The no 6 shirt became his property and he held it until the claims of Alistair Robertson, whose signing was announced two days after the win over Everton, could be resisted no longer. Kaye went on to amass 361 Baggies appearances and was named Midland Footballer of the Year for the second time in 1970 - the year he lined up alongside John Talbut again in the League Cup Final. With Hull, he made 72 League appearances. He was to remain friends with his Wembley adversary Alan Ball and even made a competitive return to the twin towers when, as joint manager, he helped Brigg Town lift the 1996 FA Trophy final thanks to a 3-0 victory against Clitheroe.

John Kaye in the latter 1990s.

Graham Lovett, having played in the FA Cup Final after recovering from a career-threatening car crash at Christmas, 1966, had the sympathy of the football world as he suffered further crushing misfortune. After playing 23 First Division games for Albion in 1968-69 and lining up in all five of the ties the club played in an impressive Cup defence that reached the semi-final stage, he was cut down, unbelievably, by another road smash in the summer of 1969. He didn't play again until the following March and the 21 League appearances he made in 1970-71, some of them at right-back, were to prove his sad swansong at The Hawthorns. In the course of eight years' service, he had totalled 156 first-team games but left his many admirers wondering what might have been. A trio of outings on loan at Southampton in 1971-72 included an ironic 8-0 defeat away to Albion's 1968 Wembley victims Everton and the man dubbed in the mid-1960s as the new Duncan Edwards retired at the age of 26 via a spell with non-League Worcester, his appalling injuries having caught up with him.

Ian Collard was yet another member of Albion's famous 1968 FA Cup winning team who didn't stay around for long after the elation of Wembley. He played only another 19 League games for the club in addition to the first three ties of the club's Cup defence before he moved on to Ipswich in the summer of 1969 in a player-plus-cash exchange with Danny Hegan. His final appearance tally in Albion colours was 97, almost 30 of them in the cups, and, having played against DOS Utrecht in 1966 in the club's first-ever European tie, he enjoyed another career highlight at Portman Road. By now bearded, he faced Real Madrid home and away in the 1973-74 UEFA Cup as the East Anglians went through 1-0 on aggregate before losing on penalties to Locomotiv Leipzig in the following round. Collard, whose brother Bruce played for Scunthorpe, turned out in 92 League games for the Suffolk club and later served them as a coach, having played a solitary one match during a loan stint at Portsmouth in which his sudden retirement came about because of the discovery of arthritis in his hip. His later travels included a spell coaching with Graham Williams in Kuwait, six years

Ian Collard.... pictured in recent years still striving to keep himself in good shape - and succeeding.

in Kentucky and Iowa as a football coach and a stint at Ipswich's Academy until the winter of 2002-03 when he switched to a high school in the town.

Jeff Astle, already in an exclusive band of players to score in every round of the FA Cup, became the first player to score in the finals of both the FA Cup and League Cup when, in the latter, he climbed above Joe Corrigan to head the opening goal of Albion's 2-1 Wembley defeat against Manchester City in 1970. His glorious FA Cup trot continued when he converted a rare penalty in a 3-0 home win against Norwich in the third round of the 1968-69 competition but he took a back seat as Asa Hartford and Ronnie Rees scored in the victory at Fulham in the next round. Astle followed up his haul of 35 goals in 1967-68 with 26 the following campaign and 30 in 1969-70, his fabulous strike rate earning him a place in Sir Alf Ramsey's squad to go to the 1970 World Cup finals after he had made his international debut against Wales at Wembley. Mexico proved to be a watershed in his career because he was well adrift of Tony Brown in the club's marksmen list in 1970-71 with 16 and notched only two the following campaign at the start of the chronic injury problems that plagued his last seasons at The Hawthorns. All told, he played 361 matches for his second and final Football League club, scoring 174 goals.

Bobby Hope was proof that, if Old Father Time didn't account for Albion's Wembley heroes, Don Howe did. Alan Ashman's successor decided there was no place in his plans for the brilliant inside-left, who never got his dream move to Rangers. He still lives in the West Midlands and was short-changed by his winning of only two senior international caps. But he continued to turn on the style at club level despite the emergence of fellow Scot Asa Hartford. Hope played 35 League games in 1968-69, 38 in 1969-70 and 34 in 1970-71, then Howe came in and the figure was down to 22 the following season. Hope's type was replaced by more functional operators during the dour years of life under his former Hawthorns team-mate and he joined newly-promoted Birmingham for £66,666 in the summer of 1972. At St Andrew's, he added another 34 League matches to the 403 (42 goals) he had played in all competitions for Albion. He subsequently played a further 42 for Sheffield Wednesday in 1976 and 1977 and brought the curtain down on his playing career with Philadelphia Atoms, Dallas Tornado and Bromsgrove, the last of whom he also served as manager at a time when he ran a post office near Sutton Coldfield.

Clive Clark badly injured his knee thanks to an appalling challenge on him during the at-times vicious post-Wembley tour of Africa and was never the same player again. The win over Everton proved to be his last appearance in the

FA Cup for the club and he appeared only 17 times in the League in 1968-69 (two goals) and was transferred the following June back to QPR, where he clocked up another seven League matches, with only one goal. Nine goals in 71 games followed with Preston as they won the Third Division title in 1970-71 under the management of Alan Ball's father and he scored one in seven with Southport before he descended, via Telford, Washington Diplomats, Dallas Tornado, Philadelphia Fury and Skegness Town, to retirement in 1976-77. Clark, living in North Yorkshire and dogged in recent years by poor health, has his place in Hawthorns history as one of Albion's most prolific-ever wingers, his tally of 353 first-team matches (301 in the League) bringing him the terrific tally of 98 goals. After retiring, he coached youngsters at Butlin's in Filey but a series of personal tragedies affected his health and it was one of the sadder stories from the 1968 squad when the Sunday Mercury revealed several years ago the possibility of him selling his Cup winners' medal.

Dennis Clarke had felt unsettled at The Hawthorns even during the latter stages of the victorious FA Cup run and says now: "I suppose I risked participation at Wembley by telling Alan Ashman I was unhappy. It's the sort of thing you do when you are young but you would pull back from in later years. I did think I was getting a raw deal, even though we had two international full-backs in Doug Fraser and Graham Williams, but I look back now and think how marvellous it was to play in the Cup Final, even as a substitute." Clarke, who was later to make millions in business and then virtually lose the lot, played only 27 first-team games for the club in total. He subsequently headed north to Huddersfield in 1969 and played 175 League games for them despite missing a year after snapping his ankle ligaments while chasing George Best in a game at Old Trafford. He then played 14 games back in the West Midlands with Birmingham before an injury suffered at Wolves a week before the FA Cup semi-final against Fulham in 1975 ended his career at the age of only 26. Early in 2003, he emigrated to Spain.

Kenny Stephens was another for whom the Hawthorns curtain fell soon after Wembley. Overlooked for the FA Cup Final, he wasn't seen in the first team again and moved on to neighbours Walsall later in 1968 following only 27 senior appearances and three goals for Albion. At Fellows Park, he managed only seven outings but was much more used back in his native West Country as he totalled 225 League appearances for Bristol Rovers from 1970-77 despite having the unusual experience of being sent off along with his former Albion team-mate Doug Fraser in a Saddlers v Rovers game. He also played 60 League games for Hereford from 1977-79.

Eddie Colquhoun, badly injured at Newcastle a few weeks before Wembley, was to play only two more games for the club - against Nottingham Forest in both the League Cup and the League in the space of four days the following autumn. His departure, though, after only 54 Albion appearances was the prelude to the best years of his career as he joined Sheffield United and played no fewer than 363 first-team games for them in a stay spanning 12 seasons. He also added nine full caps to his Scottish under-23 honours before spending five years in American football with Detroit Express and Washington Diplomats and embarking on a busy life outside the game that has included five years as a hotelier in Northumberland, a spell as a newsagent/post office manager near Rotherham and, now, the role of manager of a private members' bar in the Yorkshire town of Conisbrough.

Nick Krzywicki continued to flit in and out of Albion's side after missing out on selection for Wembley 1968. He had a few games as a centre-forward but had still amassed only 64 appearances for the club when he was sold by Alan Ashman in 1970 to Huddersfield, where he played another 47 games up to 1973. He also went on to win eight full caps, memorably beating Gordon Banks with a shot as he scored his only international goal in a 1-1 draw against England at Cardiff's Ninian Park in April, 1970. His career wound down at Scunthorpe (on loan), Northampton (81 League games) and Lincoln (55), the latter of whom he served under Graham Taylor and played in a thrilling 3-2 FA Cup defeat at The Hawthorns in 1975-76. The quickest thing on two legs at The Hawthorns for many years, he later saw his daughter make her name as a cross-country international and his son become professional at Elland Golf Club in Yorkshire.

Rick Sheppard's impatience for first-team football led to him leaving The Hawthorns in 1969 although he had come in as an injury-enforced replacement and played eight of the first nine League games in the August and September following the FA Cup Final. Having totalled only 54 matches for the club, including 11 in the League Cup, he moved back to his home city and joined Bristol Rovers. There, he added a further 151 League appearances to his record and also had two games on loan for Torquay in 1973-74, the latter after a fractured skull suffered in action for Rovers in January, 1973, had hastened his retirement. With sad coincidence, he died in the same 1998-99 season in which Albion fans mourned the passing of his goalkeeping rival John Osborne.

Alan Ashman joined Greek giants Olympiakos two weeks after his sacking from Albion and inspired them to a runners-up finish in the league in his only season there. It was almost inevitable that he would return to Carlisle at some stage and he did so in 1972. In his second season back, he led them to the top flight for the first time in their history. They went straight down again and their popular manager moved on to Workington and, following a spell as a scout at Manchester United, into the Walsall hot-seat. Coaching or scouting postings followed at Derby, Hereford, Plymouth, Notts County, Mansfield, Derby again and Telford as he remained in the West Midlands, passing away at his Walsall home late in 2002.

Stuart Williams followed his Hawthorns stint by rejoining Southampton as assistant to manager Lawrie McMenemy. He later had coaching or management spells at Aston Villa, Morton and in Norway and Iran. He is now settled in Hampshire in retirement after running a bed-and-breakfast establishment in Southampton, where he and wife Carole had Dennis Wise and ex-Manchester United and Saints striker Ted MacDougall among their residents.

Subscribers

Bryan R Adams

Dylan J Adams

Ray and Mike Anstis

Keith Archer

Nick Archer

Stuart Arms

Rob W Arnold

Gary K Ashman

Annette and Bob Babington

Scott Edward Baggott

Richard Ball

Sidney Bate

Martin Banner

Roy Bannister

Matthew Bastable

Dave and Peter Baxendale

Ron A Beards

Ronald Beardsmore

Steve Bell

Rob Bishop

George Blackham

Ian Blackham

Clive Blake

P J Blocksidge

Tony Bridges and family

Robin Brittain

John G Brown

Stuart Bullock

Rod Burton

Raymond Stuart Cannon

Stephen Carr

Jon Carter

Ian M Cartwright

Darren Cooper

John and Hannah Court

Andy Cutler

Joseph Dangerfield

Paul Davis

William Barry Dawes

John Dickinson

Andrew Dodd

Joseph Eaton

B R Evans

Edwin Evans

John Finn

Anthony Fisher

Colin Fletcher

Heather Gibbons

Terry Gibbons

Ray Gibson

Maurice Goodwin

James Robert Grainger

Steve Gregory

Graham Grice

David Grigg

Ronald Grigg

Ben Hall

Geoff Hall

Robin H Harman

Mick Harrison

Jane Haycock

Barbara and Roy Hayden

John Hickman

Christopher Hickmans

David Hollingmode

Gil Holmes

Michael and Matthew Holton

Ian Robert Homer

John Homer

Joseph Anthony Homer

Brian Horton

Ian Hoult

Graham Jackson

Lynn Jackson

Ron Jarratt

Brendan Jones

Craig Robert Jones

Richard Jones

Mike Kerry

John Edward King

Ray Lawrence

Cathy and John Maddox

Paul Malley

Daniel Marshall

Kev, Helen and Jack Martin

Laurence Martin

Gordon Maull

Geoff May

Philip Millard

John Monkton

Mike Moren

Stuart Mowat

Bill Mynott

Claude and Ann Mynott

Steve Mynott

Geoff Nevey

John R Nicholls

Roy Nicholls

Christopher T Nock

Thomas Nock

Charlotte and Lucy Norridge

Gina and Jon Norridge

Christopher M O'Brien

Walter T O'Brien

Philip Owen

Andrew Patrick

Mike Phipps

David Pick

Laurie Rampling

John Ray

Andy Roberts

Jonathan Clive Round

Julian Rowe

Carl Ruston

Archie Ryan

Mark Edward Selwood

Barry Shermer

Bob Skelding

Holly Skidmore

J T Skidmore

Natasha Skidmore

Steve & Terryann Skidmore

Derek Smart

Clive William Smith

Robert Smith

Steve Sorrill

David Spicer

Stan Sunley

David J Taylor

Barbara A Tout

Jonathan Joseph Tranter

Paul Tranter

Brian W Trevis

Ian Tubby

Ken and Val Turbutt

Peter Turner

Tony Turner

Paul Veness

Robert Veness

Frank Vidler

William Waite

Terry Wall

B P Walters

Jonathan Peter Want

Shaun J Wellings

George Wheatley

Andy Whitehouse

Derek Whitehouse

Geoff Whitehouse

Mark and Taylor Whitehouse

John Williams

Paul N Williams

Terry Wills